PRAISE FOR THIS BOOK

"This book presents the state-of-art of longitudinal network analysis. It is comprehensive while staying concise, well structured, and clearly written. Definitely a moneyball in the field!"

—Weihua An, *Emory University*

"A brilliant 'how to' for modelling dynamic network data. An exquisite balance of model intuition, assumptions and practical advice, accessible to all network/data scientists."

—Alexander John Bond, *Leeds Beckett University*

"This is a very timely book that provides critical skills for conducting explanatory analysis of longitudinal social network data. Both beginners and advanced analysts can benefit from reading this book as it provides many real-life examples, illustrating computational processes, interpreting results, and even furnishing R codes. For those who aspire to learn advanced topics in analyzing longitudinal social network data, this is a must-have book."

—Song Yang, *University of Arkansas*

Longitudinal Network Models

QUANTITATIVE APPLICATIONS IN THE SOCIAL SCIENCES

SERIES: QUANTITATIVE APPLICATIONS IN THE SOCIAL SCIENCES

Series Editor: Barbara Entwisle, Sociology,

The University of North Carolina at Chapel Hill

Longitudinal Network Models

Scott Duxbury
University of North Carolina at Chapel Hill

Los Angeles | London | New Delhi
Singapore | Washington DC

Los Angeles | London | New Delhi
Singapore | Washington DC

FOR INFORMATION:

SAGE Publications, Inc.
2455 Teller Road
Thousand Oaks, California 91320
E-mail: order@sagepub.com

SAGE Publications Ltd.
1 Oliver's Yard
55 City Road
London EC1Y 1SP
United Kingdom

SAGE Publications India Pvt. Ltd.
B 1/I 1 Mohan Cooperative Industrial Area
Mathura Road, New Delhi 110 044
India

SAGE Publications Asia-Pacific Pte. Ltd.
33 Pekin Street # 02-01
Far East Square
Singapore 048763

Copyright ©2023 by SAGE Publications, Inc.

ISBN 978-1-0718-5773-1

Acquisitions Editor: Helen Salmon
Associate Editor: Yumna Samie
Production Editor: Aparajita Srivastava
Copy Editor: Gillian Dickens
Typesetter: Integra
Cover Designer: Candice Harman
Marketing Manager: Victoria Velasquez

This book is printed on acid-free paper.
22 23 24 25 26 10 9 8 7 6 5 4 3 2 1

CONTENTS

SERIES EDITOR'S INTRODUCTION

It is with great pleasure that I introduce *Longitudinal Network Analysis* by Scott Duxbury. Its focus is the analysis of changes in network structure and their potential impact on behavior. Readers familiar with regression and social network analysis will welcome a clearly written and accessible introduction to this advanced field. Professor Duxbury is ideally positioned to write this volume as he is an active contributor to the methodological literature on longitudinal network analysis.

Chapters in *Longitudinal Network Analysis* cover popular models for network panel data, temporal exponential random graph models and stochastic actor-oriented models; models for relational event data, including relational event models and a brief introduction to the dynamic actor network model; and network influence models when the dependent variable is an actor's behavioral attribute, both the temporal network autocorrelation model and coevolution models (an extension of SAOM). Each makes assumptions about the temporal duration of a tie (whether long-lasting as in the case of a friendship or "of the moment" as might characterize a purchase in Saturday's farmers' market), the causes of tie change (specifically, the degree to which the creation or activation of ties is understood to result from a decision by the relevant actor(s)), the sequencing of tie changes (especially the temporal precision of measurement), and the generative processes of interest. They differ in whether the focus is actors, ties, or network influence. The choice among them is guided by theoretical as well as methodological considerations.

The volume strikes a perfect balance between high-level thinking and the practical details of application. Each chapter begins with an overview of the specific method under consideration. Then, in a section titled "the intuition," it zooms out to show how the method resembles approaches readers already know (e.g., logistic regression, Cox models, the generalized linear model). Readers will appreciate the review of assumptions that follows, especially Professor Duxbury's comments on their reasonableness and which are most critical to the success of the method. After a formal presentation of the statistical model, Professor Duxbury provides a fully worked example, including the motivating question, data preparation, model specification, interpretation of results, and model checking. The examples are friendship formation among Dutch college students, drug purchases on the dark web, and network influences on adolescent smoking and drinking behavior. Data and code to reproduce these examples are available on the companion website at

https://study.sagepub.com/researchmethods/qass/duxbury-longitudinal-network-models. Along the way, Professor Duxbury comments on software and utilities currently available and when analysts would need to write their own source code.

Longitudinal Network Analysis is at the forefront of a rapidly evolving field. It includes a comprehensive list of up-to-date references. In each chapter, the explanation of the modeling approach concludes with specific recommendations about relevant technical literature that readers might wish to consult. The volume's concluding chapter identifies and discusses areas of active methodological development, including missing data (especially on ties), measurement error, unobserved heterogeneity, and challenges associated with scaling up to networks with large numbers of actors. Professor Duxbury provides guidance for how readers should proceed with these issues based on current wisdom while at the same time cautioning that future advances might modify this advice. With this volume in hand, readers will be well equipped to analyze change in social networks, including the components, determinants, and consequences of this change.

—*Barbara Entwisle*
Series Editor

ACKNOWLEDGMENTS

To Dana and Dave, who have contributed immeasurably to this book through their mentorship. If the quality of tutelage counted toward authorship, this book would be cited as Haynie, Melamed, and Duxbury (equal contributions from the first two authors, of course).

To Jenna, my incredible wife, who has never wavered in her support during every challenge and every triumph. I hope that you enjoy the many "gwesps" in the following pages.

SAGE and the author are grateful for feedback from the following reviewers during the development of this text:

- Weihua An, *Emory University*

- Alexander John Bond, *Leeds Beckett University*

- Martin Bouchard, *Simon Fraser University*

- Anthony Paik, *University of Massachusetts–Amherst*

- David Schaefer, *University of California, Irvine*

- Zachary C. Steinert-Threlkeld, *University of California, Los Angeles*

- Song Yang, *University of Arkansas*

ABOUT THE AUTHOR

Scott Duxbury is an assistant professor of sociology at the University of North Carolina at Chapel Hill. His methodological work focuses on statistical network analysis and panel data analysis. He has designed diagnostics for statistical network models, outlined methods for comparing coefficients between statistical network models, and developed a class of panel models that deal with unobserved time heterogeneity. His studies have appeared in *Sociological Methods & Research*, *Sociological Methodology*, and *Network Science*. Scott's applied work examines criminal network dynamics and reactions to external disruptions, as well as racial conflict and the politics of punishment. It has appeared in outlets such as *American Sociological Review*, *American Journal of Sociology*, *Social Forces*, *Social Problems*, *Criminology*, *Socio-economic Review*, and *Social Networks*.

CHAPTER 1. INTRODUCTION

Network science has recently enjoyed enthusiasm from a wide range of disciplines. From physics to computer science to public health and the social sciences, scholars want to know how and why things are connected. The recent influx of interdisciplinary funding for social networks studies is perhaps unsurprising, as many agencies want to stake a claim to the emerging field of network science. Nor is it necessarily surprising that network methods are increasingly viewed as the cutting-edge in many scientific fields. Yet buried in the enthusiasm, funds, and theorems of network methods lies a dilemma. Although longitudinal social network data are increasingly collected, there are few guides on how to navigate the range of available tools for longitudinal network analysis. The applied social scientist is left to wonder: Which model is most appropriate for my data? How should I get started with this modeling strategy? And how do I know if my model is any good? This book answers these questions. It surveys the lay of the land in longitudinal network modeling to provide a "how-to" on longitudinal network analysis.

Network data represent relationships. In principle, any relational data set can be represented as a network. Statistical network analysis is distinct from classical regression in that the central interest of a statistical network model is *interdependency*. While a core assumption of regression analysis is that observations are independent, longitudinal social network data measure connections between people and changes in those connections over time.

Longitudinal network models provide social scientists with a tool for analyzing *change* in relational data structures and how changes in network structure influence the behaviors of social agents embedded in evolving networks. Longitudinal network methods can answer a variety of questions related to structural network contexts and their effects on network dynamics. Sociologists and social psychologists, for instance, have a rich history examining how network structure influences status processes and friendship ties in small group settings (An, 2015b; Goodreau, Kitts, & Morris, 2009; Kreager et al., 2017; Lewis & Kaufman, 2018; Block, 2015; Schaefer, Kornienko, & Fox, 2011). Criminologists and public health scholars evaluate how network processes affect adolescent risk behavior, like drinking, unprotected sex, and smoking (adams & Schaefer, 2016; Ragan, Osgood, & Feinberg, 2014). Scholars of organizational studies and economics evaluate how and why structural network characteristics lead actors to choose specific exchange partners (Granovetter, 1985).

What This Book Covers

Longitudinal Network Models takes stock of the current literature on statistical analysis of longitudinal network data. It assumes that the reader is at least passingly familiar with network measurement, description, and notation and is versed in regression analysis but likely unfamiliar with statistical network methods. The goal of the book is to guide such readers toward choosing, applying, assessing, and interpreting a longitudinal network model. It seeks to provide a bridge from the excellent introductory texts like Wasserman and Faust (1994), Yang, Keller, and Lu (2016), Knoke and Yang (2020), and Newman (2010) to the more technical literature on longitudinal network methods.

What This Book Does Not Cover

Limited attention is given to methods that do not predominate the social sciences. Block models, latent space models, and various Bayesian and/or nonparametric extensions to the modeling strategies discussed here are not reviewed in depth. Many of these models have, of course, been applied with interesting results in the social sciences (Coutinho, Diviak, Bright, & Koskinen, 2020; Padgett & Ansell, 1993). But they are not the norm. To that end, the book uses social scientific language. "Vertices" or "nodes" are referred to as "*actors*," while "edges" are referred to as "ties." Further, this book is primarily concerned with *statistical* methods for longitudinal network analysis. It does not review descriptive statistics, clustering algorithms, or community detection methods. Interested readers may find it helpful to consult Newman's (2010) introduction to network analysis, much of which gives attention to descriptive methods, or Cranmer, Desmarais, and Morgan (2021) for a general introduction to inferential network analysis. For a primer on network data collection, please see adams (2019).

The Path Ahead

Each chapter is organized with a specific data structure or research question in mind. Chapters 2 and 3 introduce the two most commonly used models for network panel data: temporal exponential random graph models (TERGM) and stochastic actor-oriented models (SAOM). Each chapter focuses on how assumptions about the nature and timing of network change inform the behavior and interpretation of each model.

Chapter 4 introduces relational event models (REM). Relational event data are distinct from network panel data in that connections between actors are activated with varying intensity and occupy only discrete, ephemeral moments in time. Chapter 5 introduces models for social influence where the outcome of interest is change in actors' behaviors or attitudes. The chapter reviews autocorrelation models as well as coevolution models that treat network selection and behavioral influence as interdependent processes.

Chapter 6 looks forward to future developments in longitudinal network modeling. As a rapidly growing field, many of the current best practices in longitudinal network analysis are imperfect. Chapter 6 discusses areas of statistical network analysis that are still "under development." The goal of this chapter is to foreshadow emerging issues that practitioners should keep in mind as the field continues to grow.

In each chapter, I provide reproducible examples implemented in R. The examples make use of the most widely used packages for statistical network modeling: statnet, RSiena, rem, and btergm. Code and data for each example can be found in the online supplement.

The remainder of this chapter reviews basic network notation and introduces theoretical and statistical issues that underlie the analysis of longitudinal network data. To the reader who is well versed in such considerations, you may want to skip ahead to later chapters. To the reader who is new to network data and analysis, the rest of this chapter is written with you in mind.

What Are Longitudinal Network Data?

Network data are represented by connections between n actors in an $n \times n$ adjacency matrix Y. Connections between actors are regarded as a random variable, where the goal of statistical network analysis is to detect the stochastic processes that give rise to each tie. We denote dyads as ij pairs of actors i and j. If the ij dyad is connected by a tie, then $y_{ij} = 1$; otherwise, $y_{ij} = 0$. In undirected networks where an ij tie reflects the presence of a ji tie, there are $\frac{n(n-1)}{2}$ possible ties; in directed networks where $y_{ij} \neq y_{ji}$, there are $n(n-1)$ possible ties.

Longitudinal network data depart from cross-sectional network data by incorporating repeated measurements. Say we have measured Y twice over two panels. Now our networks are $Y^{t=1}$ for the first panel and $Y^{t=2}$ for the second. Our unit of analysis is no longer the dyad but the dyad panel ijt, indicating the measurement of the ij dyad at each panel observation. Hence, our central interest in longitudinal network analysis is *change* in the tie activity between network measurements. We seek to statistically evaluate why ties form, why ties dissolve, and how tie dissolution and tie formation influence the behaviors of actors embedded in evolving networks.

Managing Longitudinal Network Data

Scholars who have worked with network data in the past know that network data management can be a challenge. Data structures can quickly become memory intensive and difficult to work with on standard computers. These issues are compounded in longitudinal settings where there are repeated measurements of each network and actor.

The most common longitudinal network data structure is the block adjacency matrix. Rather than an $n \times n$ adjacency matrix, we stack the adjacency matrices for each observation to create an $nt \times nt$ data matrix. Imagine a simple network of three actors. Our cross-sectional adjacency matrix would look something like this:

$$\begin{bmatrix} & 1 & 2 & 3 \\ 1 & 0 & 1 & 0 \\ 2 & 1 & 0 & 0 \\ 3 & 0 & 1 & 0 \end{bmatrix}.$$

Now say we've measured the network twice. We combine the two adjacency matrices into a single block matrix:

$$\begin{bmatrix} & 1_{t=1} & 2_{t=1} & 3_{t=1} & 1_{t=2} & 2_{t=2} & 3_{t=2} \\ 1_{t=1} & 0 & 1 & 0 & 0 & 0 & 0 \\ 2_{t=1} & 1 & 0 & 0 & 0 & 0 & 0 \\ 3_{t=1} & 0 & 1 & 0 & 0 & 0 & 0 \\ 1_{t=2} & 0 & 0 & 0 & 0 & 1 & 1 \\ 2_{t=2} & 0 & 0 & 0 & 0 & 0 & 0 \\ 3_{t=2} & 0 & 0 & 0 & 0 & 1 & 0 \end{bmatrix}.$$

We can regard the block matrix as containing four distinct adjacency matrices in four separate "blocks." The first block in the upper-left quadrant is the cross-sectional adjacency matrix from earlier. The bottom-right block is the adjacency matrix representing our second network measurement. The off-diagonal blocks are empty because it is impossible for ties to connect two panels.

The block-adjacency matrix is the most convenient data structure for fitting statistical models. However, it is not the most convenient data structure for storing network data. Even small increases in the number of repeated measurements or the number of actors yield exponential increases in data size. For the purposes of storage, then, block matrices are often unappealing.

One of the more common structures for storing network data is the edgelist. For a cross-sectional matrix, we create an $ij \times 2$ matrix, where the first column indicates the set of actors i and the second column contains the set of actors j:

$$\begin{bmatrix} i & j \\ 1 & 2 \\ 2 & 1 \\ 3 & 2 \end{bmatrix}.$$

The benefit of this structure is that we only record existing ties, so we greatly reduce memory demands by excluding all "0s." This can be especially useful in longitudinal network analysis, since each off-diagonal block is empty. The edgelist is straightforward to use for longitudinal network storage by including a third column recording the time period. For instance, if we convert the block matrix above into edgelist format, we obtain

$$\begin{bmatrix} i & j & t \\ 1 & 2 & 1 \\ 2 & 1 & 1 \\ 3 & 2 & 1 \\ 1 & 2 & 2 \\ 1 & 3 & 2 \\ 3 & 2 & 2 \end{bmatrix}.$$

It's clear to see that edgelists greatly reduce demands on computer memory. While the block matrix has 36 cells, the edgelist only has 18. We've cut the storage requirements in half. Due to these advantages, edgelists are probably the most popular structure for storing longitudinal network data.

So what about actor attributes? For all the complexities network data introduce for repeated measurements, we get very few additional difficulties when it comes to storing actor attributes. As in other panel data, we simply record time-varying and time-invariant actor characteristics by treating the actor panel as the observation. Then all we have to do is link the ego and alter characteristics at each time period to the network data. Similarly, it is easy to record edge and dyad characteristics by expanding on the data structures above. We again create either a block matrix or edgelist. But instead of recording the presence or absence of a tie in each cell, we record the dyad or edge covariate of interest.

Modeling Capabilities

The core benefit of longitudinal network models is the ability to account for and statistically evaluate interdependence. All longitudinal network models reviewed in this book are able to represent the effects of actor characteristics, dyad characteristics, multiplex network ties, endogenous network structure, and certain types of temporal dependence.

- **Actor characteristics** are actor-level variables such as race, age, education, and gender. Their inclusion in a statistical network model reflects the tendency for actors to be more active in creating or dissolving outgoing or incoming ties when they possess a specific attribute. Kreager et al. (2017), for instance, examine status nominations in a prison inmate network, finding that older inmates tend to be most frequently nominated as "powerful or influential" by other inmates.

- **Dyad characteristics** are attributes of each *ij* pairing in a social network. The most common examples of dyad characteristics are *homophily* and *heterophily*, the former of which refers to the tendency for actors who are similar on some social attribute (race, sex, income) to be connected, while the latter refers to mixed attribute connections. Schaefer et al. (2011), for instance, study depression homophily in the AddHealth friendship network data using SAOM. They show that depression homophily emerges because *nondepressed* peers avoid depressed peers, rather than depressed peers seeking out one another for friendship.

- **Multiplex** network ties refer to those ties that exist in multiple measures of network relations. A classic example is provided by Granovetter (1985), who famously argued that economic relations tend to occur between actors who are already connected by social relations. Here ties are multiplex because dyads are connected by *both* social and economic relations.

- **Endogenous sources of social change** are perhaps the crowning achievement of statistical network models (Robins, Pattison, Kalish, & Lusher, 2007; Snijders, 2001). Longitudinal network models are able to determine whether the *structure* of social networks contributes to changes in social ties. Network structural characteristics are computed on the network to represent specific structural configurations that increase or decrease the likelihood of a tie. Papachristos, Hureau, and Braga (2013), for instance, document the structural influence of two paths in gang violence relations. Two paths form in gang violence networks when gang i shoots a member of gang j after being shot at by gang k. In gang violence networks, two paths reflect pecking orders, where gangs must preemptively strike against other gangs after being shot at so as to not appear weak. Papachristos et al.'s (2013) results reveal that the *network structure* of gang violence is a powerful predictor of gang warfare.

- **Temporal dependencies** may also exist in longitudinal network data. Ties may be dependent on ties that existed in the past, or they may form as part of an emergent structure within the same time period. Consider the case of cooperation in small group settings. Actors may create strategic coalitions in between rounds that emerge as cohesive clusters in unison. Alternatively, actors may forge ties based on historical patterns of cooperation, such as by creating ties to actors with whom a focal actor has cooperated in the past. This former type of temporal dependence is referred to as *within–time period dependence*, while the latter represents *between–time period dependence*. As we'll discuss in the coming chapters, some models, like TERGM, allow for flexible specification of between– and within–time period dependencies, while other models like SAOM and REM are limited to only between-period dependencies.

- **Influence processes** are one of the more common foci for social science researchers. Although the trend in network methods is toward analyzing the processes that generate network structure, many practitioners are primarily interested in analyzing how network structures influence characteristics of the actors in a network. We may want to know how social capital in the form of network connectedness influences wages or hiring (Mouw, 2006), or we may want to know whether triad structures help to insulate actors from suicide ideation or depression (Schaefer et al., 2011). In these cases, we are less concerned with modeling network dynamics and more concerned with accounting for how network structures influence individual outcomes. In Chapter 5, we'll see how ordinary regression models can be expanded to control for network dependencies and allow for modeling of network influence processes. We'll also see how SAOM can be expanded to model network and behavior change as simultaneous processes of selection and influence.

Why Not Standard Regression?

Because network modeling creates additional complexities beyond what we typically encounter in regression analysis, it is important to understand why regression is typically inappropriate for longitudinal network data. Network data pose important problems for statistical inference. Placing network data and measures into a linear or generalized linear model can problematize statistical inference. This is for two reasons.

The first reason is because of nonindependence. Recall one of the first regression assumptions: Data are independent and identically distributed. We assume that the spacing between each observation is uniform and that measurements of a given observation are not influenced by other observations. We derive our degrees of freedom for a standard statistical test as $df = n - k$, where k is the number of parameters in a model. In an ideal world where the *only* regression assumption violated is nonindependence, this problem produces autocorrelated errors in a regression model. If autocorrelation is the only issue, our coefficients are unbiased but we do get downward biased standard errors. This is plain to see if we revisit the equation for standard errors in an ordinary least squares regression:

$$SE_\beta = \sqrt{\frac{\sum_{i=1}^{N}(y_i - \hat{y}_i)^2}{df} \cdot n \frac{1}{\sum_{i=1}^{N}(x_i - \bar{x})^2}}. \tag{1.1}$$

If data are not independent, then we have fewer degrees of freedom than assumed, meaning that our standard errors should be larger than we estimate.

This is more or less the best-case scenario in a network analysis using standard regression: The only problem that we encounter is downward biased standard errors and inflated assessments of statistical significance. However, the more commonplace scenario is that some network process, such as homophily, popularity effects, or peer influence, is at work. If this is the case, then we need to measure the network process and include in a model. When a network tie is the dependent variable, however, we are unable to include many informative network processes on the right hand of the equation. This is the second issue that we encounter: simultaneity bias, which affects both coefficients and standard errors.

Simultaneity bias is a case of endogeneity bias where the outcome causes the input variable at the same time that the input causes the outcome. Imagine that we want to predict the probability of observing a tie as a function of the number of triangles using a generalized linear model. The relationship between the number of triangles and the probability of observing a tie would be endogenous: The independent variable (triangles) is a mathematical function of the dependent variable (ties). This type of simultaneity bias can be severe in many settings. To analyze network data, we need models that provide unbiased estimates of endogenous network effects and their variances.

An important point to highlight is that the statistical issue of representing network data and the theoretical issue of accounting for interdependence are intertwined. We cannot subvert the problems implicated in modeling network data by simply excluding network measures, such as peer effects, degree centrality, or triads, from our model. In these cases, while we do not introduce simultaneity bias, we introduce a new form of endogeneity bias via omitted variables. It is well established that network substructures usually exert powerful influence over tie formation. Indeed, by going through all the extra steps of collecting complete network data, we are assuming that there is something about the structure of the network worth capturing. In these cases, we cannot get around the complex statistics of network analysis by excluding network measures. We need to use a model that can include network variables, even if only to draw valid statistical inference from exogenous attributes.

Thus, although nonindependence is common within certain data structures, such as nested data used for multilevel models or in serially correlated longitudinal data, what makes the problem unique in network analysis is that we are *interested* in nonindependence. There is no convenient workaround to handling this type of nonindependence, such as including frailty terms or detrending the data. Many of the complexities involved in network analysis arise not from the fact that the data are nonindependent but instead from the fact that we are attempting to study the very facets of our data that violate core regression assumptions.

If statistical analysis of network data was not already complicated enough, the introduction of repeated measurements increases complexity even further. Repeated measurement data present the possibility of serial correlation, nonstationarity, and spurious trending that threaten inference in classical panel data analysis. And it is often the case that tie changes go unobserved between network measurements. Each of the modeling strategies discussed in this book provides novel solutions to the problem of statistical interdependence in longitudinal network data. Each solution, in turn, proceeds from ontological assumptions about the nature of a tie, the timing of tie changes, and the underlying change process. Consequently, a characterizing feature of longitudinal network analysis is that *theoretical* considerations, rather than statistical considerations alone, must guide model selection.

Theoretical Issues

In addition to the modeling capabilities and statistical issues that inform model selection, a core feature of longitudinal network models is ontological assumptions about the nature of tie changes. Each of the models in this book make distinct assumptions about (1) the temporal duration of a tie, (2) the causes of tie change, (3) the sequencing of tie changes, and (4) the generative processes of interest.

What Is a Tie?

A critical consideration when modeling longitudinal network data is what exactly it means for actors to be connected and what exactly it means for those connections to change. It was once common to simply aggregate network ties over time frames to create cross-sectional network data sets. Since the advent of the Internet and systematic data collection from administrative records, we are increasingly presented with network data with fine-grained information on the timing of tie changes. Whereas once researchers were content to say "a friendship exists or it does not," they are increasingly asking, "What constitutes a friendship?" "Can friendships be reduced to binary measurements?" and "Are friendships simply aggregations of high-frequency repeated events?" (Butts, 2009; Kitts, 2014).

The answers to these questions are often not clear but have pushed forward an array of new modeling strategies. The network panel models discussed in Chapters 2 and 3, for instance, assume that ties occupy relatively long-lasting temporal moments. Because tie changes are "coarse"—that is, it takes a long time to change a tie—we are able to re-create the change process with relatively crude information on timing obtained from network panel observations. In contrast, REM (discussed in Chapter 4) assumes rich information on timing. Relational events are discrete interactions that occupy brief temporal moments and are activated varying intensity across repeated observations (think golf games, business meetings, phone calls). These "ties" do not persist across temporal moments in the same sense as "coarse" social ties, like kinship or friendship.

Why Do Ties Change?

A second ontological issue is the question of *why* a tie changes. This might seem like a silly question. The point of a statistical network model is to evaluate why a tie changes! But the question is very relevant. Longitudinal network models are derived under assumptions about what—or who—drives tie changes. When these assumptions are violated, it is possible to obtain well-behaved statistical models that tell us nothing about the data.

For instance, "tie-based" models, including TERGM and REM, are relatively agnostic about the causes of tie changes (Butts, 2017). But this agnosticism has been critiqued for providing an overly simplistic representation of network change processes, unrealistic assumptions about the stability of the network over time periods and emergent properties of the network between observation periods, and limited attention to the role of social agents ("Change we can believe in: Comparing longitudinal network models on consistency, interpretability, and predictive power", n.d.; Block, Stadtfeld, & Snijders, 2019; Stadtfeld, Hollway, & Block, 2017a). In contrast, "actor-based" models, like SAOM, assume that outgoing tie changes are forged and withdrawn by boundedly rational actors. Actors are given opportunities to alter ties, and network change is the outcome of such opportunities (Snijders, 1996, 2001).

The assumption of agent-driven change is not applicable for some networks, and assumptions about boundedly rational behavior must be deployed with careful consideration. This extra set of assumptions also introduces a great degree of complexity in terms of model formulation, estimation, and large-sample behavior. But this complexity is paid back in many ways by a wide array of modeling utilities unavailable in tie-based models. For instance, the coevolution models discussed in Chapter 5 are able to model the simultaneous, endogenous evolution of networks and actors' behavior (Steglich, Snijders, & Pearson, 2010). Actor-based models are also able to model multivariate network outcomes—simultaneous change in multiple networks—while tie-based models are not (Snijders, Lomi, & Torló, 2013).

Choosing a tie-based or actor-based model carries important consequences for statistical inference. Assumptions regarding the tie- or agent-based nature of network change are nonfalsifiable. Hence, estimating an actor-based model erroneously may provide you with a well-fitting, statistically significant model full of substantive nonsense. Alternatively, estimating a tie-based model when the underlying data-generating process is actor driven can provide you with a set of results that fundamentally misrepresent the underlying network change process. The decision on which model is most appropriate can only be made using substantive knowledge.

When Do Ties Change?

A third consideration is the question of timing. Panel data include repeated measurements of the same units. The timing between each observation may be constant or may vary between time periods. In standard longitudinal data analysis, the question of unobserved changes is usually a minor issue, with perhaps the exception of survival analysis. This is because we are working within the realm of independence. We can assume that the within-unit variation contains all the relevant information on timing, and we assume that the passage of time is conditionally independent of change in the time-varying variables.

When working with network data, this implicit assumption becomes much more problematic. If we do not know when a tie changed, then we do not know when network structures changed or how they changed. Most dramatically, we don't know what the network structure was at the time of a tie change. If our argument is that ties form within triads, but we can't measure whether a given tie actually closed a triad at the time that it formed, then we are limited in our ability to test our theoretical argument.

Each of the dynamic models discussed in this book presents a distinct solution to this type of problem. TERGM, for example, assumes that the representation of each network at a given time period is reflective of the dynamic processes that generated it. In other words, we assume that the variation in the network structure at each observation is reflective of the underlying processes that generated the structure in between observations. SAOM, by contrast, uses special simulation procedures to impute the unobserved sequence of tie changes. To do so, it makes a relatively strong assumption on the agent-based nature of tie changes and actors' motivations for changing ties. REM addresses the same issue by assuming we have perfect measurement of the timing of each tie change.

Each model is restricted in its ability to re-create the timing of tie changes. If there are large time windows between observations, then the TERGM assumption that unobserved changes are noninformative is likely untenable. On the other hand, if the nodes in the network are not "actors" or it is unreasonable to expect agent-driven change, then SAOM will return uninterpretable results. REM is the most flexible model in terms of accounting for sequencing but is also the most demanding in terms of data requirements.

Do We Care About Tie Changes at All?

A final consideration is whether tie changes are even of interest. Many research questions relate to network influence on individual outcomes. In these cases, the generative models for network structure, like REM and TERGM, will not answer the research question. Chapter 5 discusses models for network influence, including network autocorrelation models and extensions to SAOM. While both models can be used to examine influence, each model may be more or less appropriate for the research question at hand. Network autocorrelation models, for instance, make no explicit assumption on the timing of tie changes or on the sequencing of tie changes, making them fairly robust to diverse data structures. In contrast, although SAOM makes strong assumptions about temporal dependencies and agent-driven change, it also allows researchers to model the *coevolution* of behavioral and tie change. This modeling capability is not available through any other method. Hence, researchers will need to determine whether the interdependence between network and behavioral change is of substantive interest or whether network change is a statistical issue that only needs to be controlled.

Summary

Model selection in longitudinal network analysis differs from classical regression in that it is first and foremost theory driven. There is no analogy to the Hausman test that can guide model selection in the presence of specific correlation structures. The good news is that there is a wide range of models available to handle possible longitudinal network data structures. The bad news is that each of these models is typically complex and there are few resources available to researchers providing guidance on how to decide which model is most appropriate for which type of research question. This book is dedicated to aiding in this type of decision.

Accompanying Website

A website for the book at **https://study.sagepub.com/researchmethods/ qass/duxbury-longitudinal-network-models** includes data and code to replicate the examples in the book.

CHAPTER 2. TEMPORAL EXPONENTIAL RANDOM GRAPH MODELS

Back in the early 1990s, a number of clever researchers got together to write a grant. While this was not remarkable in itself, the grant writers happened to be interested in networks. They proposed to collect a large-scale probability sample of schools in the United States. What's more, they proposed to collect the romantic and friendship ties among students.

The study, of course, was the Longitudinal National Study of Adolescent to Adult Health, or "AddHealth." AddHealth has become one of the most widely used data sets in the social sciences. The AddHealth network data is a staple data set in longitudinal network analysis. With two waves of network panel data on multiple schools and almost complete in-school network coverage, the AddHealth network data continue to be relatively unrivaled in terms of scope and depth of information on network ties and actor characteristics.

AddHealth showed researchers how longitudinal network data could be collected. Respondents could be interviewed at multiple moments in time and asked about their social relations. The change between network panels could be modeled as a statistical outcome. The spate of developments in network panel data analysis in the late 1990s and early 2000s emerged either with AddHealth data in mind or using similar school-based network data collection efforts that were based off of the AddHealth framework (Snijders, 1996, 2001; Van De Bunt, Duijn, & Snijders, 1999).

The AddHealth data are emblematic of network panel data structures. Tie measurements are "coarse," meaning that there are imprecise data on when exactly a tie changes. The ties of interest are also reasonably assumed to be long-lasting. This chapter introduces a common model for network panel data analysis, the temporal exponential random graph model (TERGM).

What Are Network Panel Data?

Network panel data contain multiple measurements of the same set of actors over time. The unit of analysis is the dyad panel, ijt. Network panel data are usually collected through survey administration. Consider the example of friendship networks. Researchers interview respondents and ask them to list five or so friends or to circle the names of their five or so closest friends from a roster. The entire network of friendship ties can then be reconstructed by

t=1   **t=2**

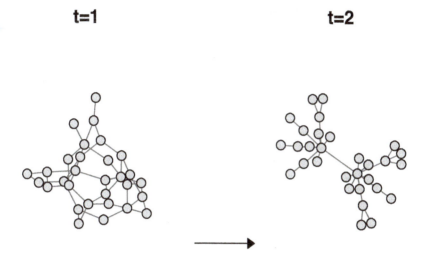

Figure 2.1 Simulated network panel data

linking each actor's responses to one another and storing their nominations in an adjacency matrix.

Network panel data differ from other forms of longitudinal network data in that they provide "coarse" tie measurements. Each network panel offers a single snapshot of the dynamically evolving network, but the tie changes between panel measurements are unobserved. Consider the simulated network panel data in Figure 2.1. Clearly, the network structure consolidated between measurements. But while we are able to measure the network at two points in time, we don't know in what order ties changed, how long each tie lasted, or why any tie changed at a given moment. This uncertainty about the nature of unobserved change means that we have to make assumptions about the ordering of tie changes and its effects on the network change process.

The temporal exponential random graph model (TERGM) is an autoregressive framework for modeling ties changes between network panels. The model is a *discrete time* model. This means that changes between network panels are regarded as discrete shifts between network states. TERGM is a minor extension of the cross-sectional exponential random graph model (ERGM). Hence, to introduce TERGM, we begin with a brief review of cross-sectional ERGM.

The Cross-Sectional ERGM

ERGM is a cross-sectional model for network structure. Say we have a single measurement of a network in the adjacency matrix Y. Our goal is to statistically evaluate why we observe this particular network structure as opposed to some other possible network configuration. To do so, we write the probability of observing Y as a function of network, actor, and dyad characteristics:

$$Pr(Y|\theta) = \frac{exp(\theta^T z(x,y))}{c(\theta)}. \tag{2.1}$$

The left-hand side of the equation is the probability of observing the network out of all possible networks that we *could* observe given a fixed set of actors. We represent the relevant variables of interest as network statistics $z(x,y)$, where $z(.)$ is a mapping function that calculates relevant network structural characteristics on y (triangles, two-stars, brokerage) and on the exogenous actor and dyad characteristics provided by our input data x (race, sex, homophily). The parameter weights for each network statistic are contained in the parameter vector θ. $c(\theta)$ is a normalizing constant that ensures that the sum of the probabilities across all possible networks equals 1.

It turns out that the calculation of $c(\theta)$ is intractable on modern computers except for case studies examining very small networks (Hunter, Handcock, Butts, Goodreau, & Morris, 2008; Vega Yon, Slaughter, & de la Haye, 2021). Consequently, the model is typically estimated by sampling a very large number of possible networks using a Markov chain Monte Carlo (MCMC) algorithm (Geyer & Thompson, 1992; Snijders, 2002). The neat result is that if we sample a very large number of networks, then the maximum likelihood of the MCMC sample approximates the maximum likelihood estimate of the model in Equation 2.1.

The Intuition

If the model in Equation 2.1 seems foreign, the good news is that we can simplify it greatly. ERGM can be represented as a logit model:

$$log(\frac{Pr(Y_{ij} = 1|Y_{-ij})}{Pr(Y_{ij} = 0|Y_{-ij})})) = \theta^T \delta_{ij}^+ (x,y). \tag{2.2}$$

This representation is an exact reexpression of the earlier model, but we replace the mapping function $z(.)$ with the *change* statistics $\delta_{ij}^+(.)$ that measure the increase or decrease in network statistics when a focal Y_{ij} tie changes from 0 to 1 and Y_{-ij} indicates that all other ties are unchanged.

This model should look familiar. It is almost an exact replica of logistic regression. Indeed, the model is an *autologistic* regression that shares the exact functional form of the more familiar logit model but is distinct in that it includes endogenous network statistics on the right-hand side of the equation (Besag, 1972, 1974; Frank & Strauss, 1986). When endogenous network statistics are omitted, the model above reduces to logistic regression (Holland & Leinhardt, 1981; Strauss & Ikeda, 1990). Hence, for all the complexity introduced by ERGM, it often helps to remember that, without sacrificing *too* much complexity, the model can be thought of as almost identical to a logistic regression. The sole difference between ERGM and logistic regression arises in models where endogenous network statistics are included on the right-hand side of Equation 2.2.

This formulation also makes clear why nonindependence in ERGM cannot be addressed by simply using a multilevel framework. While nesting each dyad in each actor with a cross-classified structure helps (Box-Steffensmeier, Christenson, & Morgan, 2018), many actors are themselves nested in higher-order substructures. If we include triadic closure and two-stars into our model, for instance, each actor is nested in a series of two-stars that, themselves, are nested in a number of embedded triangles. This problem only grows more complex as we add higher-order structures. Degree distributions, for instance, are network-level measures. Even a simple model including only two-stars, triad closure, and the degree distribution would imply a nesting structure where each tie is nested in two actors, who are each nested in a distinct set of two-stars, which are nested in a distinct set of triangles, and which are nested in a network. This type of nesting structure is not only complicated to specify but varies idiosyncratically for each individual network under study and each model specification.

As in standard logistic regression, the parameter vector θ is interpreted as the increase or decrease in log-odds of realizing a tie given a one-unit change in corresponding network change statistic. For exogenous characteristics, we can state that increases in a covariate are associated with higher log-odds of being connected to other actors. For endogenous characteristics, we can state that increases in the *change* in a given network statistic correlate with a higher likelihood of observing a tie. Say we are examining a network of between-hospital patient transfers as a function of triadic closure and the number of hospital beds (Kitts, Pallotti, Lomi, Quintane, & Mascia, 2017). A positive value for the number of hospital beds would tell us that a hospital is more likely to be engaged in patient transfer as the number of available beds increases. A positive coefficient for triadic closure would tell us that as the number of closed triangles increases between two hospitals, so too does the likelihood that those two hospitals will be involved in patient transfer.

A unique capability of ERGM is that we can also interpret coefficients at the macro-level (Besag, 1974). This is plain to see by recognizing that the same parameter vector appears in both Equations 2.1 and 2.2. We can therefore interpret θ as increasing or decreasing the probability of observing *an entire network*. In the case of hospital transfers, for instance, we could conclude that increases in the count of hospital beds across all hospitals increase the likelihood of observing our particular hospital-transfer network out of all possible hospital-transfer network configurations. We could also state that increases in the number of triangles increases the probability of observing our particular network. Although this interpretation is used less frequently in applications (Desmarais & Cranmer, 2012a), it is available for both cross-sectional and temporal ERGM (Block et al., 2019).

Assumptions

ERGM makes several assumptions that translate into the longitudinal formulation of the model. As in other statistical models, we assume no omitted variables. However, because we have only one representation of the network, we also must assume that the network is a reasonable representation of the underlying generative process. To put that differently, we must assume that, for whatever underlying process generated our network data, our network data are not a highly unlikely outcome of that process. The network statistics act as the target statistics for maximum likelihood estimation, where the estimator is the set of parameter values that minimize the difference between predicted network statistics and the measured statistics. The likelihood estimator and method of moments estimator are equivalent in ERGM (Snijders, 2002).

Temporal Exponential Random Graph Models (TERGM)

Very little additional complexity is introduced when moving from ERGM to TERGM. TERGM is a discrete time autoregressive model first proposed by Hanneke, Fu, and Xing (2010). The model is autoregressive in that we control for correlations between network panels to examine only the *change* between network panels. To estimate TERGM, we stack the waves of network data into a single $nt \times nt$ block matrix, where t indexes a network measurement. The diagonal blocks are the $n \times n$ adjacency matrices for each wave, while the off-diagonal blocks are structural 0s. Recall from Chapter 1 that our block matrix should look something like this:

$$
\begin{bmatrix}
 & 1_{t=1} & 2_{t=1} & & i-1_{t=t} & i_{t=t} \\
1_{t=1} & 0 & 1 & \cdots & 0 & 0 \\
2_{t=1} & 1 & 0 & \cdots & 0 & 0 \\
\vdots & \vdots & \vdots & \ddots & \vdots & \vdots \\
i-1_{t=t} & 0 & 0 & \cdots & 0 & 1 \\
i_{t=t} & 0 & 0 & \cdots & 1 & 0
\end{bmatrix}.
$$

We then simply estimate an ERGM predicting the block matrix while controlling for dependencies between network states. Let $\mathbf{Y^t}$ be a stacked block matrix of $T-1$ network panels, where T is the number of network panels in the data, and let $\mathbf{Y^{t-1}}$ be a block matrix of $T-1$ network panels lagged by one panel observation. We write TERGM:

$$
Pr(\mathbf{Y^t}|\theta, \mathbf{Y^{t-1}}) = \frac{exp(\theta^T z(x, \mathbf{y^t}) + \psi \mathbf{Y^{t-1}})}{c(\theta, \mathbf{Y^{t-1}})}. \tag{2.3}
$$

The model is exactly equivalent to the earlier model, but now we include the lagged network $\mathbf{Y^{t-1}}$ that controls for all connections at $t-1$. ψ is the autoregressive parameter for the lagged network, usually specified as an offset parameter constrained to equal 1. By including this offset parameter, we hold constant all between-panel consistencies. This is the same workaround used for nonstationary time series data when employing a random walk model (e.g., ARIMA(0,1,0)). What this means is that we can interpret coefficients as influencing the probability that a tie will *change* between repeated measurements.

The Intuition

As in the cross-sectional ERGM, we can express TERGM as an autologistic regression,

$$
log\left(\frac{Pr(Y_{ijt} = 1|Y_{-ijt})}{Pr(Y_{ijt} = 0|Y_{-ijt})}\right) = \theta^T \delta_{ijt}^+(x, \mathbf{y^t}) + \psi \mathbf{Y^{t-1}}_{ij}. \tag{2.4}
$$

This means that like ERGM, TERGM is closely related to the more familiar logistic regression and, in special cases where endogenous network effects are excluded, reduces to logistic regression during estimation (Almquist & Butts, 2014). As opposed to cross-sectional ERGM, the unit of analysis here is the dyad panel, rather than the dyad. Hence, the change statistics $\delta_{ijt}^{+}(.)$ are time varying, reflecting the increase or decrease in network statistics at a given time period. $\mathbf{Y^{t-1}}_{ij}$ is an indicator variable recording whether an *ij* tie existed at $t - 1$. We interpret θ as influencing the log-odds of a network tie *changing*, where negative coefficients indicate lower likelihood of a network tie forming and positive coefficients indicate an increased probability of a network tie forming between panels.

Assumptions

Because TERGM is a special case of ERGM, TERGM makes all of the same assumptions described above but also includes several additional assumptions related to the network change process. TERGM is a Markovian model, meaning that the model assumes that all of the information relevant to a network change process is contained in the preceding network panel. This assumption is often misinterpreted to mean that delayed processes are impossible, for instance, that the model assumes that the network structure at $t - 2$ is irrelevant. This is not the case. Rather, the Markov assumption means that any information on a lagged time process must be represented in the model. A more appropriate way to think about the Markov assumption is that there is no higher-order, unmeasured dependencies between network states. If a tie at $t - 2$ influences a tie at t in a way that is not captured in the model through the lagged network or parameterized network statistics, then parameters and standard errors may be affected.

The model is also a *discrete time* model. We assume that the time it takes for a tie to change is less relevant than the order of network change between panels. Because TERGM makes no explicit assumption on the ordering of tie changes, the model also implicitly assumes that the *sequence* of unobserved tie changes between network panels is not confounded with the observed changes—that is, that the ordering of tie changes is adequately represented by the discrete shifts measured between each network panel. This means that if there are large bouts of tie activity between network panels, the predictive performance of TERGM typically suffers (Block et al., 2018).

Model Specification

TERGM offers a suite of modeling terms that can be used to specify endogenous and exogenous network processes. As a member of the ERG family of models, TERGM is able to incorporate a plurality of informative statistics. Table 2.1 presents a number of commonly used network statistics.

Term	Formula	Lower-Order Terms
Undirected		
Node matching	$\sum_{i<j} y_{ij} a_i a_j$	Node (a)
Node mixing	$\sum_{i<j} y_{ij} a_i b_j$	Node (a,b)
Two-star	$\sum_{i,j} y_{ij} y_{ik}$	
Triangle	$\sum_{i,j} y_{ij} y_{ik} y_{jk}$	Two-star
Directed		
Node matching	$\sum_{i<j} y_{ij} a_i a_j$	Sender (a), receiver (a)
Outgoing node mixing	$\sum_{i<j} y_{ij} a_i b_j$	Sender (a), receiver (b)
Incoming node mixing	$\sum_{i<j} y_{ij} b_i a_j$	Sender (b), receiver (a)
Reciprocation	$\sum_{i<j} y_{ij} y_{ji}$	
Reciprocal node matching	$\sum_{i<j} y_{ij} y_{ji} a_i a_j$	Sender (a), receiver (a), reciprocity, node matching
Reciprocal node mixing	$\sum_{i<j} y_{ij} y_{ji} a_i b_j$	Sender (a,b), receiver (a,b), reciprocity, incoming node mixing, outgoing node mixing
Two-path	$\sum_{i,j} y_{ij} y_{jk}$	
Out-two-star	$\sum_{i,j} y_{ij} y_{ik}$	
In-two-star	$\sum_{i,j} y_{ij} y_{kj}$	
Three-cycle	$\sum_{i,j} y_{ij} y_{jk} y_{ki}$	Two-path
Transitive triplet	$\sum_{i,j} y_{ij} y_{ik} y_{kj}$	Two-path, in-two-star, out-two-star

Table 2.1 Common ERGM terms. y is a tie variable, and a and b are nodal attributes.

The node-matching term is an exogenous dyad characteristic used to represent *homophily* in social networks—the tendency for two actors to be connected when they share some relevant attribute (race, gender, education). The node-mixing term is the inverse specification for *heterophily*. The triangle term in Table 2.1 represents the prevalence of triadic structures in undirected networks. A common example of triadic influence in social networks is the preference for actors to befriend friends-of-a-friend, where i and j are more likely to be friends if both actors are friends of k.

Table 2.1 also presents statistics for *directed* networks. Directed networks broaden the scope of available network statistics. For instance, homophilous ties may or may not be reciprocated, and the tendency for reciprocity, where ij ties are also ji ties, may influence the interpretation of homophily terms. Also of note are the multiple types of triad structures in directed networks (Holland & Leinhardt, 1971). Whereas triad structures are uniform in undirected networks, the directionality of triads can influence interpretation. For instance, *three-cycles* are triad structures where each actor receives and sends exactly one tie; the connections travel from i to j, from j to k, and from k to i. The asymmetry of three-cycle structures is often interpreted as reflecting a propensity toward status processes, and adversity to three-cycle formation in friendship networks is often interpreted as reflecting a lack of status processes (though, see Block [2015] on this interpretation). The *transitive triplet* is still another triadic structure, comprising one outgoing two-star, one incoming two-star, and one two-path.

The interpretation of each network statistic must be made with context in mind. For instance, while Papachristos et al. (2013) interpret adversity to transitive triplets as evidence of few functional alliances in gang violence networks, transitive triplets are similarly interpreted as evidence of status-based nominations in influence networks (Kreager et al., 2017) and as a peer effect in friendship networks (Block, 2015). Hence, while the same statistics can be calculated on any network panel data set, the *meaning* of those statistics varies dramatically depending on the empirical context.

A third point to consider in Table 2.1 is *nesting structure*. Most network statistics are "nested in" higher-order statistics (Snijders, Pattison, Robins, & Handcock, 2006). For instance, a single undirected triangle is composed of three undirected two-stars. This nesting structure means that we must control for lower-order terms in our models to interpret the network statistic of interest. For instance, if we do not control for two-stars in a model that includes triadic closure, we cannot determine whether a positive triad coefficient reflects the tendency for ties to close triangles or a tendency for ties to extend two-stars. This is the exact same problem that is encountered in regression analysis when interactions are included into a model, but main effects are omitted.

Within or Between Time Dependence?

A key utility in TERGM unavailable in other network panel models is the ability to specify both within- and between-panel dependencies. Consider the statistics in Table 2.1. The default behavior in most software, such as btergm and stergm, is to specify *within*-panel dependencies. We would compute each statistic on the block adjacency matrix and estimate the model. If we are interested in triadic closure, for instance, the coefficient would tell us whether an *ij* tie is more or less likely to form between waves if it emerges as part of a complete triangle. If we want to detect whether actors are more likely to form ties as part of a coalition between rounds of repeated games, we might expect within-panel dependence.

Oftentimes, however, we are more interested in *between*-panel dependence. We want to know whether a tie is more likely to form if it closes a previously open triangle. This implies that we are not interested in the effect of network statistics at time t but at $t - 1$. We can also specify this type of between-panel dependence in TERGM, although sometimes it requires additional programming. btergm, for instance, allows us to compute a *delayed* reciprocity statistic, which tells us whether a directed tie is more likely to form at t if it reciprocates an incoming tie at $t - 1$. This is often the interpretation that we want.

The good news is that this type of model is actually far easier to estimate. If we only specify between-panel dependencies, then we obtain the sequential exogeneity of network measurements, and the model reduces to logistic regression. The bad news is that delayed network effects introduce a lot of complexity, and so software isn't well developed. Consider the case of closing a directed triplet in a three-panel data structure. We could expect that an *ij* tie is more likely to form if it closes an *jk* to *ki* directed two-path. But we might also expect that the triplet is likely to form in a particular sequence, where the *jk* tie forms at $t = 1$, the *ki* tie forms at $t = 2$, and the *ij* tie forms at $t = 3$. This introduces a fair amount of complexity in terms of programming the network statistics, and so current software offers limited utilities for specifying between-panel dependencies. It is for this reason that scholars sometimes contrast TERGM with stochastic actor-oriented models (SAOM) on the grounds that TERGM assumes within-panel dependence while SAOM assumes between-panel dependence (Block et al., 2019, Block et al., 2018; Cranmer et al., 2021; Schaefer & Marcum, 2017). This distinction is one that is typically true in practice but is not necessarily true in theory. Practitioners *could* specify between-panel dependencies within a TERGM framework if they are willing to write new sourcecode. For time-varying exogenous attributes, however, it is straightforward to specify between-panel dependence by simply lagging exogenous attributes.

Example 2.1. A TERGM Analysis of Friendship Formation Among Dutch College Students

Social scientists are often interested in small group processes. Why do people become friends with one another? And how does peer context influence friendships? These are the kinds of questions TERGM is ideally suited to answer. To get at these questions, we will use the friendship network data collected by Van De Bunt et al. (1999). The data are available for use via the networkDynamicData package in R. The data contain seven network panels of friendship nominations among 49 Dutch college students. The students were first interviewed upon college entry and were reinterviewed at 3- to 6-week intervals. Because some students dropped out and some did not respond to more than four survey panels, the data are limited to only the friendship ties connecting 32 students who answered at least four survey panels and remained in college throughout the study.

Students were asked to rank their relations on a scale of 1 to 5, where 1 indicated a close friendship, 2 indicated a friendship, 3 indicated a friendly relationship (pleasant contact but not necessarily a "friend"), 4 indicated a neutral relationship, and 5 indicated a negative relationship. For the analysis to follow, we code the network such that friendship ties exist between students if they scored between a 1 and a 3 on the relationship measure and do not exist otherwise. We will treat the network here as directed, although it is sometimes the case that social scientists focus on bidirectional ties in friendship networks (Goodreau et al., 2009; Lee & Butts, 2018). Code to replicate this example is provided in the Chapter 2 supplement.

Data Preparation

The networkDynamicData package provides us with a preformatted data set as a dynamic network object. Oftentimes we do not have a cleanly packaged data structure to start out with. The most common strategy for handling dynamic node and network data in R is to use arrays. We can get the array of dynamic networks using the get.networks function in networkDynamics. This returns a list of each individual network panel as a distinct network object. A simple way to manage network data is to store the adjacency matrix for each network panel in a sequentially ordered list. Then, to convert the adjacency matrices into network objects for analysis, it is as simple as looping over each entry of the list and using the as.network function in statnet.

We can use a similar procedure to assign node or edge attributes. After each adjacency matrix has been converted into a network object, we can use the %v% operator to assign node attributes or %e% operator to assign edge attributes. Example code to convert the Van De Bunt network from a list of adjacency matrices into network objects and to assign node attributes to each panel is provided in the Chapter 2 supplement.

Specification

Once we've prepared our data, we formulate the TERGM to represent the social processes that influence friendship. For this example, we will be using the R packages networkDynamicData to access the data, statnet for data management and cleaning, ergm and btergm for model estimation, and btergm and ergMargins for diagnostics and interpretation.

First we specify *actor* characteristics, including sender and receiver effects for gender and smoking behavior. These terms tell us whether students are more likely to be nominated as a friend (receiver effect) or nominate other students as friends (sender effect) when they are female as opposed to male or when they smoke regularly. Second, we consider the tendency for similar students to befriend one another. We specify undirected homophily terms for smoking behavior and gender. These terms take a value of 1 if two students share the same smoking behavior or the same gender and are equal to 0 otherwise. Third, we'll specify sender, receiver, and homophily effects for continuous actor attributes using the length of each student's schooling program. The sender and receiver effects are specified similar to the gender and smoking terms, but now our homophily measure is the absolute difference between the sender program length and the receiver program length. For instance, if the sender and receiver are in the same length program, the absolute difference statistic will have a value of 0. If the sender is in a 2-year program and the receiver is in a 4-year program, the absolute difference statistic will have a value of 2. The key distinction between this statistic and the matched nodal attribute is that lower values indicate *higher* similarity. Hence, if we hypothesize that there should be homophily, we would expect the coefficient for the absolute difference to be negative.

Finally, we consider endogenous network effects. We'll examine both between- and within-panel network dependencies. Our first network effect is *reciprocity*, referring to the tendency for student i to nominate j as a friend if j also nominates i as a friend. We specify this term as delayed reciprocity, lagged by one observation period (Leifeld, Cranmer, & Desmarais, 2018). This is a between-panel dependency since the statistic is computed on prior network states. The statistic takes a value of 1 if j has nominated i as a friend as of the *previous* time period $(t - 1)$ and is equal to 0 otherwise. We also include a triadic structure term. Here we will use a geometrically weighted edgewise shared partnership term (GWESP), which is a weighted triad statistic that typically improves MCMC convergence over unweighted statistics (Hunter, 2007). A positive coefficient indicates a positive effect of triadic closure on tie formation. This is a within-panel dependency, meaning that we interpret the measure as reflecting whether ties are more likely to form when they emerge as part of a complete triad between panel observations. Finally, we will also include a geometrically weighted indegree term (GWIDEGREE). This statistic preserves the indegree distribution of the network.[1]

Interpretation

The TERGM results are presented in column 1 of Table 2.2. The edges parameter is analogous to the intercept in logistic regression. The parameter is $- -9.18$, meaning that the probability of a tie forming between network panels is .0001 ($logit^{-1}(-9.18) = .0001$) when all covariates are held at 0. The receiver effect for gender indicates that, compared to male students, female students have 2.77 ($exp(1.02) = 2.77$) times higher odds of receiving new friendship nominations between waves. Turning to smoking parameters, there is evidence that nonsmokers receive fewer ties than smokers. Inversely, nonsmokers tend to nominate more alters as friends compared to smokers. There is little evidence that similar smoking behavior influences friendships.

There are also strong program effects. Increases in program length are associated with decreases in incoming friendship ties and increases in outgoing friendship ties. The absolute difference parameter for program length is negative, telling us that as students become more similar in terms of program length, they are more likely to form friendship ties.

The endogenous network effects tell us whether network structure influences students' friendships. The delayed reciprocity parameter indicates that the odds that i will nominate j as a friend are roughly three times greater ($exp(1.07) = 2.92$) when j has nominated i as a friend at some point in

---

[1] Both GWESP and GWIDEGREE are specified with fixed tuning parameters of .7.

1. TERGM MCMC MLE estimates	
Edges	−9.18*** (.516)
Female	
Receiver	.90*** (.096)
Sender	.16 (.102)
Same	.15 (.088)
Nonsmoker	
Receiver	−.34*** (.055)
Sender	1.05*** (.070)
Same	.10 (.063)
Program	
Receiver	−.167*** (.045)
Sender	.480*** (.049)
Absolute difference	−.212*** (.047)
Reciprocity$_{t-1}$	1.09*** (.074)
GWESP	3.07*** (.245)
GWIDEGREE	−4.02*** (.491)

Table 2.2 TERGM of the Van De Bunt network using MCMC maximum likelihood. Coefficients and standard errors reported.

Note: MCMC = Markov chain Monte Carlo; MLE = maximum likelihood estimation; GWESP = geometrically weighted edgewise shared partnership; GWIDEGREE = geometrically weighted indegree distribution.
***$p < .001$.

the past. The GWESP term tells us about triadic structure. Because the GWESP term is a *within*-panel term, we interpret the coefficient to mean that the odds that a friendship will form between waves are 27 times higher ($exp(3.30) = 27.11$) when the friendship emerges as part of a complete triangle between waves, with diminishing returns to each triangle closed. There are two key elements to this interpretation. First, the triangle *emerges* between waves; that is, it refers only to situations where i, j, and k are disconnected at $t - 1$ but are each connected at t. Second, the geometric weighting of the term means that each triangle closed by a friendship receives decreasing weight. Whereas the first triangle closed by a tie increases the odds of a tie 27-fold, each additional triangle only increases the odds of a tie by a fraction of that amount.

The GWIDEGREE parameter is tricky to interpret. Usually the parameter is included only as a control for the degree distribution, rather than interpreted explicitly. The most intuitive way to think about GWIDEGREE is that it represents the shape of the indegree distribution. Larger negative values produce left skewness in the indegree distribution, while larger positive values produce greater right skewness. Interested researchers may find it helpful to use Michael Levy's Shiny app to build intuition on this interpretation. The app is available at `https://michaellevy.shinyapps.io/gwdegree/`. The app takes input values of estimated GWDEGREE parameters and returns the model-implied degree distribution(s).

Model Checking

Simulation approaches are standard for assessing goodness of fit in TERGM (Handcock, Robins, Snijders, Moody, & Besag, 2003; Leifeld et al., 2018). The basic idea behind this approach is to evaluate how well our model represents the data. If the model represents the data well, then any networks we create using our TERGM coefficients should look fairly similar to our observed network. We evaluate this by first simulating a distribution of random networks from the estimated model and then evaluating whether the interquartile range of the simulated network statistics contains the observed network statistics. If the characterizing features of our observed network—geodesic distances, triads, degree distribution—fall within the simulated distribution of network statistics, we can conclude that our model is doing a good job of representing the data.

We can calculate the goodness of fit statistics by using the gof and gof.plot functions in the btergm and ergm packages. Each panel in Figure 2.2 represents a different network statistic: the number of two-stars (dyadwise shared partnerships), triangles (edgewise shared partnerships), the undirected degree distribution, the indegree distribution, the path lengths between actors (geodesic distance), the ratio of correctly predicted ties to incorrectly predicted ties (TPR/FPR curve), and a measure of community structure (modularity). The boxplots for each panel represent the interquartile ranges for the simulated network statistics. The solid black line represents the statistics of the observed network. By most metrics, the model fits well. The geodesic distances, undirected degree distribution, and indegree distribution of the observed network fall within the interquartile range of the simulated network statistics. The edgewise and dyadwise shared partnership statistics are also reasonable, although the model overestimates the number of triangles and the number of two-stars. The TPR/FPR ratio is also strong, with relatively few incorrectly predicted ties. However, the modularity statistic is poor, indicating that the model is not recapturing community structure.

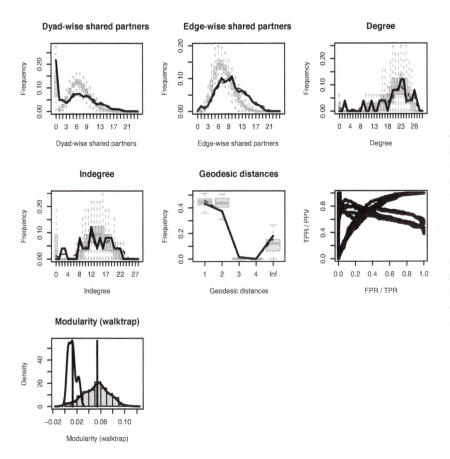

Figure 2.2 Goodness of fit for TERGM. Boxplots and histograms trace distribution of simulated network statistics ($n = 1,000$). Black line traces observed network statistics.

The next step in model checking is examining MCMC convergence. Our goal here is to verify that the MCMC algorithm has sampled a wide variety of possible networks, rather than an overabundance of networks with idiosyncratic properties. Because MCMC likelihood estimation relies on us getting a large, random sample of simulated networks, estimates from MCMC methods can be biased or unstable during model reestimations if there is not sufficient coverage of the sampling distribution. Think of it this way. If we oversample observations with large amounts of triadic closure, we will overestimate the importance of triangles in our model. Inversely, if we undersample the same observations, we could underestimate triadic effects. Further, because each MCMC sampler starts from a different location, reestimating the same model may provide us with a completely different set of results when the sampling algorithm hasn't converged but provide us with little guidance on which set of results, if any, should be trusted. In each of these cases, the primary threat to our statistical inference is that the algorithm has not returned a representative sample of networks.

We can evaluate how well the algorithm has explored the sample space by plotting the MCMC results using the checkdegeneracy function in btergm. The function gives us insight into the coverage of the MCMC sample with respect to the entire sample space of network statistics. When assessing MCMC convergence, we are looking for two things. First, we want to see if the Markov chains have "mixed." Best practice dictates that we compile the estimates from several distinct MCMC samplers to ensure that any model estimates are not unduly shaped by the behaviors of one starting location or one particular MCMC sampler. By checking that the sampling distributions overlap, we are able to verify that each simulation is obtaining a substantively similar picture of the network sampling distribution. The caterpillar plots on the left column of Figure 2.3 show these results. Ideally, each of the "caterpillars" overlaps, meaning that each Markov chain has explored a similar region of the sample space. Our TERGM generally shows good mixing for most terms, with the exception of GWIDEGREE.

Second, we are looking to see if the chains explore the entire sample space. While the first step tells us whether each MCMC sampler explored similar regions of the sample space, this second step tells us whether we have good coverage of the *entire* sample space. Ideally, the caterpillars should drift above the 0 line as well as below it. In this area, our TERGM is lacking, particularly for GWIDEGREE, GWESP, and the sender, receiver, and homophily terms for gender and smoking. It's clear that the Markov chains have gotten stuck in a particular region of the sampling distribution. This is also reflected in the density plots, where we would prefer to see each density plot in Figure 2.3 centered on 0.

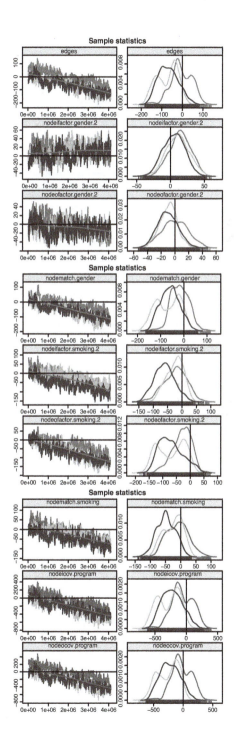

32

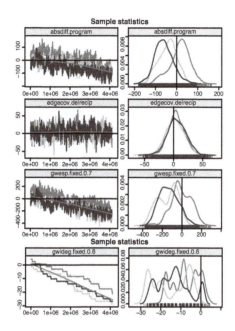

Figure 2.3 MCMC diagnostics for TERGM for four Markov chains using separate seed values. Left-hand column traces autocorrelation plot for MCMC sample; right-hand column reports density plot for MCMC sample statistics.

If we find poor mixing, there are several possible solutions. First, we can respecify the model to something more parsimonious. If the parsimonious model is well behaved and well fitting, this suggests that the problem in the earlier model is overspecification and that the parsimonious model is preferred.

Second, we can increase MCMC sample size and model iterations using the control.ergm parameter in btergm by increasing the values of the MCMC. sample and MCMC.interval parameters. These specifications increase the number of network statistics sampled and the length between each sample, respectively. In models with many parameters or large data sets, it is often necessary to manually tune the control.ergm parameter to promote convergence. In the above model, for instance, MCMC mixing is generally good and the sample space sufficiently explored for most parameters. Here, we would probably increase the size of the MCMC sample and the length of the MCMC sampling interval. If MCMC diagnostics for GWIDEGREE did not improve, we would likely exclude the term, provided that model fit did not suffer when the term is excluded.

Poor convergence is also sometimes evidence of degeneracy—a condition where the MCMC maximum likelihood estimates generate a distribution of networks that are either entirely empty or entirely connected (Handcock et al., 2003). When we encounter degeneracy, we can be reasonably certain that our model is not doing a good job of representing the data. Thus, we usually need to adjust model specification (Hunter, 2007; Snijders et al., 2006). The suite of geometrically weighted terms, such as GWESP and GWIDE-GREE, is designed to reweight structural network characteristics so as to guard against degeneracy. Thus, if our models are not converging, one of the most widely applied solutions is to respecify the model with geometrically weighted terms. A more elaborate discussion of geometric weighting and its effect on ERGM convergence can be found in Snijders et al. (2006) or Hunter (2007).

A final consideration is collinearity. Network statistics tend to be highly correlated, often at levels above .9. High collinearity in network statistics can cause nonconvergence and degeneracy, provide multiple solutions to the likelihood function, and estimate invalid standard errors. Simulation results suggest that MCMC variance estimates are generally stable as long as variance inflation factors are below 100 (Duxbury, 2021a). If collinearity is detected, we may be able to improve model fit by excluding the collinear model parameter. Variance inflation factors for TERGM parameters can be calculated using the vif.ergm function in ergMargins. The variance inflation factors are very low for the Van De Bunt school network, where the largest is 3.66 for the GWIDEGREE parameter. This is far below the threshold of 100 typically regarded as severe in ERGM applications. We can therefore conclude that collinearity is not a problem in our model.

Note that, if we do encounter collinearity, the problem can be much more severe than in classical regression. In standard regression, multicollinearity only increases the size of standard errors. In TERGM, strong collinearity can prevent the Markov chain from converging to the stationary distribution. When this happens, we can't be sure that our model has approximated the maximum likelihood. Consequently, our coefficients can be biased, our standard errors invalid, and each could change when rerunning the model. If we detect high collinearity, we can evaluate convergence by examining MCMC diagnostics and by reestimating the model to evaluate whether parameter values are stable. If our estimates are unstable or the MCMC diagnostics are poor, the best course of action is to exclude the highly collinear term. Sometimes we can also subvert the issue by increasing the size of the MCMC sample or the step length of the sampling algorithm, although this strategy is only possible for moderate levels of collinearity and will be ineffective in the presence of severe collinearity.[2]

Advanced Interpretation

Once our model is checked and we have a sense of the general patterns in our TERGM results, we can direct attention to more complex issues that arise in model interpretation. Due to its similarity to logistic regression, TERGM inherits similar problems that influence interpretation of logistic regression coefficients. In particular, it is now widely recognized that logistic regression coefficients cannot be interpreted as effect sizes, compared between models, and that interaction coefficients can be biased (Allison, 1999; Karlson, Holm, & Breen, 2012; Mood, 2010). Each of these problems also exists in TERGM (Duxbury, 2021c).[3] But, they are somewhat more prevalent in TERGM—the reason being that homophily parameters and many other commonly used dyad covariates are in fact interactions between the sender and receiver effects (Morris, Handcock, & Hunter, 2008; Snijders & Lomi, 2019). Hence, we need to use special procedures if we want to interpret interactions (including homophily and heterophily effects), compare coefficients between models, or direct attention to effect sizes.

The ergMargins package provides utilities for conducting this kind of interpretation in TERGM. The package implements the average marginal effect (AME) framework proposed in Duxbury (2021c) to evaluate effect sizes and to draw between-group and between-model comparisons. The AME is simply the mean of the gradient, or first-order partial derivative, of predicted values. It can be interpreted as the increase or decrease in the probability of observing a tie form between waves given a unit increase in independent variable. If we observe a one-unit increase in a variable such as income, the AME would tell us the increase or decrease in the probability that two nodes will be connected given that change in income.

Table 2.3 reports the AMEs for our results. To start, we can interpret the AME for the between-panel reciprocity parameter. The AME is .172, meaning that, compared to a tie that would not reciprocate an incoming tie, those

---

[2]For severe collinearity, we can't even be sure that the MCMC maximum likelihood has converged to a global maximum when parameter estimates are stable. The MCMC sampler may be stuck in a local peak.

[3]The problem arises because TERGM coefficients absorb the variance of any omitted variables, even when those variables are uncorrelated with measured variables. For details on why these issues exist in logistic regression and how they can affect parameter inference, please see Breen, Karlson, and Holm (2018). For simulation evidence on the scope of bias in TERGM coefficients, see Duxbury (2021c).

1. TERGM AMEs	
Female	
Receiver	.131*** (.025)
Sender	.032 (.024)
Same[a]	.022 (.012)
Nonsmoker	
Receiver	−.046** (.018)
Sender	.190*** (.014)
Same[a]	.018 (.013)
Program	
Receiver	−.028*** (.007)
Sender	.087*** (.011)
Absolute difference[a]	
2 to 3	.032** (.001)
3 to 4	−.013*** (.004)
Reciprocity$_{t-1}$	.172*** (.018)
GWESP	.480*** (.065)

Table 2.3 TERGM of the Van De Bunt network using MCMC maximum likelihood. Average marginal effects (AME) and standard errors reported.

Note: MCMC = Markov chain Monte Carlo; MLE = maximum likelihood estimation; GWESP = geometrically weighted edgewise shared partnership.
[a]The difference in AME when the moderating variable changes from 0 to 1. AME standard errors estimated with the Delta method.
**$p < .01$. ***$p < .001$.

ties that reciprocate incoming ties are about 17 percentage points more likely to form. This result is striking. The odds ratio for the parameter is exp(1.07) = 2.92, which is also sizable but tells us less about the change in probability. Since the edges parameter is small in column 1 of Table 2.2, it would be reasonable to expect that the actual change in probability corresponding to an increase in the odds would not be that large. By interpreting the AME, we see that the delayed reciprocity parameter has a large effect.

The next thing that we need to assess is interaction effect size and significance. Since interaction coefficients can be biased in TERGM (Duxbury, 2021c), we test interaction effects by calculating the difference between the AME at each level of a moderating variable. We first compute the sender AME for gender when the alter is male (AME = .129, $p < .001$) and the

AME for gender when the alter is female (AME = .151, $p < .001$). Next, we calculate the difference in AMEs to obtain the interaction effect. The difference in AMEs is .022 and is marginally significant at $p = .065$. This result tells us that the probability that a female student will forge ties with another student increases by about .022 when the alter is also female but is not significant. We'll do the same test for smoking behavior. Here, the sender AME for nonsmoking students is −.046 ($p < .001$) when the alter is a smoker and is .190 ($p < .001$) when the alter is a not a smoker. The interaction effect is .017 and is not significant ($p = .43$). This tells us that there is a slight but nonsignificant change in the probability that two students will become friends if they share smoking status.

The last thing we need to check is the significance of the absolute difference parameter for program length. For absolute difference parameters, the default behavior in ergMargins is to hold the main effect—here, the sender effect for program length—at its mean to evaluate moderation. Because the mean program length is 3.31, this means that we'll be evaluating whether senders are more likely to create outgoing ties to peers as they move closer or farther away from a program length of 3.31. To begin, we'll look at the AME when alters' program length is equal to 2 years. The AME is .047 ($p = .017$), meaning that the probability that a sender with an average program length of 3.31 will forge ties with another student increases by .05 when the alter is in a 2-year program. The AME, however, increases to .08 ($p < .001$) when the alter is in a 3-year program and to .05 ($p < .001$) when the alter is a 4-year program. Since the mean program length is 3.31, this result is consistent with the homophily hypothesis that as alters' program length approaches a fixed sender program length of 3.31, we are increasingly likely to see ties form.

We can now test this more formally by computing the differences in AME as alters' program length changes. The logic behind this method is that, as alters' program length approaches the mean value of 3.31, we should see the effect of alters' program length on tie formation increase. Similarly, as alters' program length moves farther away from a value of 3.31, we should see the effect of alters' program length attenuate. The difference in AMEs when alters' program length changes from 2 years to 3 years is .032 ($p < .001$) and is −.013 ($p < .001$) when alters' program length changes from 3 years to 4 years. Consistent with the homophily hypothesis, this result tells us that ties are more likely to form as alters' program length approaches the mean sender program length but decreases as alters' program length moves away from the mean sender program length. Indeed, the mean interaction effect is .009 ($p < .001$), indicating that the interaction is, on average, significantly different from 0. Collectively, these results indicate that students tend to forge and maintain connections with other students in similar length programs.

Scholars interested in asymptotic inference may wonder how to understand statistical significance in the context of TERGM. In a classical regression setup, the p value gives the probability that we could estimate a coefficient at least as large as the one we observe and have the true population coefficient equal 0. A small value indicates that it is very unlikely that the coefficient we estimate can be attributed to random error. However, because network data are interdependent, we violate random sampling principles. The data are not identically and independently distributed. How, then, do we make sense of statistical significance?

TERGM parameters provide a *process-oriented* interpretation. Process-oriented inference refers to modeling strategies that attempt to recapture the social processes that create our data. This means we can conceptualize the parameters as estimating the true homogeneous effect that gives rise to a distribution of possibly observed network change processes. In this respect, our p values represent the probability that we could estimate a TERGM coefficient from our data with the true generative coefficient being equal to 0. To put it less technically, a small p value suggests that if we were to sample a comparable set of social agents (e.g., school students) with a comparable set of social ties (e.g., friendship connections) from several distinct social settings, we should expect to find similar sets of coefficients in each setting.

Note, however, that the asymptotic sampling distributions of network statistics are not well defined. Hence, exact p values are usually less informative than standard benchmarks for statistical significance (Lusher, Koskinen, & Robins, 2013). Readers who are understandably uncomfortable with relying on statistical significance as a benchmark for substantive evaluation may find the Bayesian ERGM of Caimo and Friel (2011) or Thiemichen, Friel, Caimo, and Kauermann (2016) to be appealing alternatives to the conventional likelihood-based model. These models can be estimated using the bergm package for R. For an in-depth discussion of likelihood-based inference using TERGM, see Schweinberger, Krivitsky, Butts, and Stewart (2020) or Schweinberger and Stewart (2020).

Missing Data

Statistical network models are far more sensitive to missing data than standard regression. In general, statistical network models are fairly robust to missing actor-level data as long as all nodes are measured but are much more sensitive to missing tie data (Kossinets, 2006). A single missing tie alters the structural configuration of the rest of the network. Hence, even random missingness can produce systematic errors.

Separate procedures are typically used for handling missing data in TERGM depending on whether tie-level or actor-level data are missing. For actor-level measures, for instance, it is common practice to impute missing data using mean or mode imputation (Leifeld et al., 2018). Although mean imputation is often balked at in standard regression, we cannot use listwise deletion in a longitudinal network model. Deleting an actor produces a much more severe type of error than mean imputation (Borgatti, Carley, & Krack-hardt, 2006; Smith & Moody, 2013). Further, mean imputation tends to pro-duce conservative bias by suppressing covariance between the independent variables and dependent variable. Hence, the end result of mean or mode imputation is typically more conservative estimates for actor-level covari-ates, but we are able to avoid missing tie data, which is the central concern in longitudinal network modeling. The btergm package offers the handle-Missings function to impute the modes of actor-level missing data.

For missing tie data, procedures are much more complex. If tie data are missing truly at random, then network structures are typically well recorded and no imputation procedure is needed for small amounts of missingness (Borgatti et al., 2006). However, if the error is systematic or there is a large amount of missingness, then we encounter difficulties. One recommendation that circulates the literature is to use a Bayesian data augmentation strategy (Koskinen, Robins, Wang, & Pattison, 2013). Bayesian models are much more efficient than standard likelihood-based models, so we are able to get more information out of the incomplete data structure. This recommenda-tion is similar to recent enthusiasm for full information maximum likelihood estimation for handling missing data in structural equation models (Cham, Reshetnyak, Rosenfeld, & Breitbart, 2017).

A second recommendation is to use model-based imputation (Robins, Pat-tison, & Woolcock, 2004). In this case, we specify an ERGM predicting the presence or absence of a tie variable. We can then take the mean pre-dicted network or a range of predicted networks to impute the missing edge data. This is similar to the logic underlying standard multiple imputation strategies that predict missing values as a function of nonmissing variables. Model-based imputation has proven to be quite effective at reproducing spe-cific structural characteristics for real-world networks (Hipp, Wang, Butts, Jose, & Lakon, 2015; Krause, Huisman, Steglich, & Snijders, 2018; Smith & Moody, 2013; Smith, Moody, & Morgan, 2017). However, the method also relies upon the adequacy of the missing-data model. A model with poor predictive power may cause more problems than it solves.

Until further developments are made for missing data imputation, researchers may find it most helpful to use multiple imputation strategies to assess robustness. If an incomplete model, Bayesian model, and model-imputed model tell us the same thing, we can have some confidence in the results. If the models diverge, the most promising current method is model-based imputation on the basis of performance in comparative empirical studies (Krause, Huisman, Steglich, & Snijders, 2018; Smith & Moody, 2013; Smith et al., 2017). However, in using model-based imputation, researchers will have to pay careful attention to the theoretically implied missing-data mechanism and have confidence that their imputation model recaptures it well. Of course, the best stage to address missing data is during data collection.

Other Modeling Considerations

Sometimes network data are generated under sample restrictions that are not reflected in the model. The AddHealth network data, for instance, limit friendship nominations to five boys and five girls each. That means that any network configurations where actors have an outdegree > 10 are impossible. We can address this issue by limiting the MCMC sample space to only include networks where actors have an outdegree of 10 or lower (Krivitsky, 2017). The constraints parameter in the control.ergm function does just this. Column 1 of Table 2.4 presents results where we constrain the outdegree in the Dutch friendship network to be 5 or lower. We see that by constraining the MCMC sample, we obtain a set of parameters distinct from the unconstrained model. Hence, if we know beforehand that there is some constraint on network structure because of sample design, we get better estimates by constraining the sample space.

Another modeling consideration is computation time. TERGM estimation can often take a long time, especially in networks with many actors or data sets with many time periods. Bootstrap pseudolikelihood estimation is one possibility to speed up TERGM estimation. Desmarais and Cranmer (2012c) show that bootstrap pseudolikelihood consistently estimates the TERGM maximum likelihood in large networks. The method involves resampling from the observed network and reestimating the TERGM as a logistic regression many times. The method is extremely useful in large network data sets as it can greatly reduce computation time where MCMC maximum likelihood estimation would otherwise be prohibitive. However, researchers must use bootstrap estimation with caution. If the pseudolikelihood estimate is a poor approximate of the likelihood estimate, which is the case in small networks, the bootstrap TERGM results will be unreliable. Bootstrap estimation should be avoided for small and moderately sized networks.

	1. Original Estimates	2. Outdegree Constrained[a]	3. Bootstrap Pseudolikelihood[b]
Edges	−9.18** (.516)	−1.59 (1.15)	−5.28*** (.557)
Female			
Receiver	.90***	−.63 (.467)	.91*** (.085)
Sender	.16 (.102)	.09 (.310)	.17* (.064)
Same	.15 (.088)	.17 (.381)	.12 (.115)
Nonsmoker			
Receiver	−.34***	−1.37** (.505)	−.06 (.08)
Sender	1.05***	−.41* (.335)	1.07*** (.134)
Same	.10 (.063)	.45 (.452)	.049 (.064)
Program			
Receiver	−.167*** (.045)	−.74** (.288)	−.11 (.058)
Sender	.480*** (.049)	−.10 (.249)	.45*** (.037)
Absolute difference	−.212*** (.047)	−.96*** (.261)	−.21*** (.020)
Reciprocity$_{t-1}$	1.09*** (.074)	.59* (.301)	.94*** (.084)
GWESP	3.07*** (.245)	1.56*** (.240)	1.46*** (.207)
GWIDEGREE	−4.02*** (.491)	−2.07 (4.754)	−7.11*** (.646)

Table 2.4 TERGM of the Van De Bunt Network using alternative estimation strategies. Coefficients and standard errors reported.

Note: GWESP = geometrically weighted edgewise shared partnership; GWIDEGREE = geometrically weighted indegree distribution.
[a]Only networks with outdegree bound to be less than 6 sampled.
[b]Bootstrap pseudolikelihood estimation. Note that it is conventional to report 95% confidence intervals for bootstrap TERGM, rather than standard errors, as the bootstrap parameters may not be normally distributed. I report standard errors here to facilitate cross-model comparisons.
*$p < .05$. **$p < .01$. ***$p < .001$.

We can implement bootstrap estimation by using the btergm command in the btergm package instead of the mtergm command that we used to estimate earlier models. Here, we set R=1000, meaning that our model is estimated on 1,000 bootstrap resamples. The model takes a fraction of the time that mtergm takes to estimate. However, it's also notable that the results differ between the bootstrap and MCMC model estimates, especially for endogenous network effects. Since the pseudolikelihood estimate differs substantially from maximum likelihood estimate for GWESP, GWIDEGREE, the program receiver effect, smoking receiver effect, and the edges parameter, these results imply that the bootstrap estimates are likely less accurate than the MCMC estimates. In this case, we should prefer the MCMC maximum likelihood model.

Model Extensions

Sometimes we are less interested in interpreting network effects than we are in controlling for network effects. For example, we may be interested in whether boys have fewer friends, on average, than girls but need to control for other types of popularity effects, such as those that result from indegree centrality, to eliminate alternative explanations. In these situations, the scalability of TERGM to large network data is restrictive, as little insight is gained by specifying endogenous network effects that require MCMC likelihood estimation. Almquist and Butts (2014) introduce an autoregressive vertex process TERGM that scales well to large network data by excluding endogenous network effects. Like other autoregressive models, it includes an offset parameter for the network panel at $t - 1$. Hence, network dependence is assumed to be a nuisance parameter, and the primary research interest is in exogenous dyad and actor processes. Because the model does not specify endogenous network characteristics, it is estimated as a logistic regression. For scholars interested only in *controlling for* network effects, rather than interpreting those effects, Almquist and Butts's (2014) model may be quite useful. The model can be implemented using mtergm as before but without specifying any endogenous network effects.

In other situations, we may regard network change as an aggregate outcome of competing social processes. The causes of tie creation may not necessarily be the same things that, when absent, cause ties to dissolve. For example, school students often prefer to create friendships with other students who have shared social characteristics, such as race and gender. However, it may not be the case that shared social characteristics are likely to be the reason that those same friendships end. Krivitsky and Handcock (2014) propose a *separable* TERGM (STERGM) that accounts for such asymmetric causality. The STERGM differs from the traditional TERGM in that STERGM regards tie formation and dissolution as conditionally independent processes. A separate set of parameters is estimated for tie dissolution and tie formation, each of which tells us why ties are likely to be withdrawn and why ties are likely to be created, respectively, between waves. STERGM can be implemented using the tergm package in R as part of the statnet suite of packages.

Another utility of TERGM is that it extends in a straightforward fashion to valued tie data. Desmarais and Cranmer (2012b), Krivitsky (2012), and Krivitsky and Butts (2017) each propose ERG-family models for modeling ordinal, discrete-continuous, and continuous tie values in network data. Because the autoregressive TERGM of Hanneke et al. (2010) reduces to an ERGM fit to a block matrix, these "generalized" ERG models can be used for valued network panel data by first arranging the networks into a block matrix, as before, and second estimating a valued-tie ERGM to the pooled data structure. For the same reason, it is also straightforward to use TERGM to analyze bipartite network data (see Wang, Sharpe, Robins, & Pattison, 2009).

Conclusion

TERGM is one of the more appealing longitudinal network models due to its flexibility. It can be applied to a range of data structures that are not immediately available for alternative longitudinal network models, such as valued networks. It also can be specified to include both between- and within-panel dependencies, and little complexity is added when moving from the cross-sectional ERGM, so it fits well into more general frameworks for inferential network analysis.

At the same time, this flexibility comes at the cost of simplistic model assumptions. The assumption that unobserved tie changes are ignorable is often untenable. In many cases, the most recent network panel will not be a realistic representation of the network at the moment that a tie formed. In other cases, the assumption of discrete changes between measurements may be unrealistic if actors form and withdraw ties in short moments in continuous time. Further, network statistics are calculated at the global level, whereas researchers may be interested in an actor-level interpretation. In the next chapter, we'll see how SAOM provides an alternative framework for formulating network change processes in panel data that provide an actor-level interpretation in continuous time.

Readers interested in further reading can consult Lusher et al. (2013) for an in-depth introduction to ERGM and TERGM. Leifeld et al. (2018) also provide a guide on using the btergm package. For additional resources on TERGM interpretation, readers should consult Leifeld et al. (2018); Block et al. (2019); Schaefer and Marcum (2017); Cranmer, Leifeld, McClurg, and Rolfe (2017); or Cranmer et al. (2021). Applied examples of TERGM and its extensions can be found in Papachristos and Bastomski (2018); McMillan, Felmlee, and Braines (2020); Cranmer, Desmarais, and Menninga (2012); Ingold and Leifeld (2014); Cranmer, Heinrich, and Desmarais (2014); Almquist and Butts (2013); or Leal (2021).

CHAPTER 3. STOCHASTIC ACTOR-ORIENTED MODELS

TERGM assumes that tie changes are the outcome of an autoregressive process in discrete time, where the *order* of unobserved tie changes is irrelevant for statistical inference. This assumption may be untenable. The behaviors of social agents are often influenced by the network structures in which they are embedded, and these structures are themselves time varying. Hence, it often makes sense to prefer a model that considers the order of unmeasured tie changes in continuous time.

Stochastic actor-oriented models (SAOM) provide such a network panel model. Snijders (1996) first proposed the model that would later become SAOM with the goal of integrating social theory with statistical inference. To Snijders (2001), the problem of network change can be regarded as one of choice behavior. Looking at the roster of friendship nominations in the register of students in Van De Bunt's collegiate friendship network, it is reasonable to ask: Of the many possible friends available, why do students pick the friends that they pick instead of others? Beginning with this assumption that changes in outgoing ties are the product of choice behavior, SAOM provides a network panel model that accounts for the unobserved order of tie changes, assumes continuous time instead of discrete time, provides an agent-level instead of tie-level interpretation, and accounts for local network effects, as opposed to the global network effects formulated in TERGM.

A primary appeal of SAOM is that it provides the interpretation that we often desire and formulates network change in a manner that aligns with how we expect networks to influence the behaviors of embedded agents. These desirable properties, however, come at the cost of several stringent identifying assumptions that may not be realistic in some empirical contexts.

The Stochastic Actor-Oriented Model (SAOM)

SAOM is perhaps the most popular model for network panel data in the social sciences. SAOM formulates actors' decisions about which ties to form and which to withdraw using an objective function. Let us assume that actors are confronted with a decision about whom to befriend. The most appealing friendship, then, would be one that, if formed, would align with actors' preferences. These preferences may relate to shared recreational interests, shared gender, similar class background, or positions in network structure (i.e., whether a potential friend is a friend of a friend). Considering all possible friendships, actors are assumed to prefer the friendship that, if formed, would maximize their preferences.

This is the heart of the actor-oriented framework. Actors are assumed to evaluate possible network ties and choose to change the ties that would "benefit" them by their own evaluation. Let $s(x,y)$ be the set of statistics computed on the exogenous variables and the endogenous network that would arise *if* an actor i were to change an ij tie from 0 to 1 or 1 to 0. These statistics represent the set of actor, dyad, and network characteristics that a researcher expects to influence actors' decisions about whom to connect to. We write the objective function:

$$f_i(x,y) = \sum_k \beta_k s_k(x,y), \qquad (3.1)$$

where β are the k coefficients. The objective function can be regarded as a generalized linear model, where the coefficients tell us the weight that each actor assigns to each of the preferences represented in $s(x,y)$. The tie that increases the weighted sum across all statistics is regarded as the most appealing possible tie to the focal actor. Hence, actors are assumed to pursue the tie changes that yield the greatest increase in $f_i(x,y)$.

Under the assumption that the decision to form or withdraw a tie is one choice out of many possible tie changes, a multinomial choice model is logical (McFadden, 1974). We write the probability model:

$$\frac{exp(f_i(x,y))}{\sum exp(f_i(x,y'))}, \qquad (3.2)$$

where $\sum exp(f_i(x,y'))$ represents the summation of the objective functions for all possible tie changes *other* than the one that maximizes the objective function. The probability that an ij tie will change is

$$\rho_i \frac{exp(f_i(x,y))}{\sum exp(f_i(x,y'))}, \qquad (3.3)$$

where ρ_i is a rate function determining whether i will be given the opportunity to change a tie at a given moment. Actors may also choose *not* to change any tie if there is no possible tie change that increases the value of the objective function. In most applications, ρ_i is uniform across actors, meaning that each actor has the same probability of being offered a change opportunity (e.g., $\rho_i = 1/n$), although this assumption is easy to modify within the SAOM framework (Snijders, 2001).

The probability model above tells us *how* actors change ties when offered the opportunity to do so. But, given that changes between network panels are unobserved, how do we know *when* actors have the opportunity to change a tie? SAOM addresses this issue by considering a large number of possible network change sequences using an agent-based simulation. Actors are chosen to be offered the opportunity to change a tie according to ρ_i and are assumed to pursue the ties that maximize $f_i(x, y)$. Each tie change opportunity in the simulation is referred to as a "micro-step." Actors are provided with a minimum number of opportunities necessary to yield a set of simulated networks comparable to the observed network. By reconstructing a plausible range of possible network change sequences, the model is able to probabilistically estimate which selection mechanisms are most likely to give rise to the observed network. A key benefit of this approach is that we are able to recover the unobserved changes to network structure by imputing those unobserved change opportunities through simulation.

SAOM is typically estimated using method of moments or generalized method of moments (Snijders, 2001; Amati, Schonenberger, & Snijders, 2015), although Bayesian (Koskinen & Snijders, 2007) and maximum likelihood estimation (Snijders, Koskinen, & Schweinberger, 2010) are also available. Maximum likelihood estimation is more efficient than method of moments, but computation is typically much longer. For networks of moderate size, method of moments is generally preferred.

The Intuition

The simplest way to think of SAOM is as a generalized linear model (Snijders, 2017).[1] We can regard SAOM as entailing two general steps: imputation and estimation. In the imputation stage, a large amount of "missing data" is imputed on network change. Each "micro-step" in the agent-based simulation is an imputed observation representing an unobserved opportunity for network change. The change opportunity is missing data in the sense that opportunities for tie changes go unmeasured in network panel data.

In the estimation stage, we fit a multinomial logistic regression to the imputed data. In this respect, we can think of SAOM as a multinomial regression for unordered categorical variables where the unordered categories are the available alters with whom ego can choose to create or withdraw a connection. Hence, without sacrificing *too* much complexity, we can regard

---

[1]More precisely, it is *two* generalized linear models: one for the rate function and one for the choice function. However, since the rate function is fixed in most applications, the rate function is usually calculated as a proportion (i.e., an intercept-only model) rather than estimated as a generalized linear model.

SAOM as a multinomial logistic regression fit to a large amount of imputed data. In fact, many of the modeling assumptions that distinguish SAOM from other generalized linear models pertain to how data are imputed, rather than how the SAOM is estimated. The β coefficients can be interpreted as multinomial regression coefficients. A one-unit increases in a given covariate effect increases or decreases the log-odds that an actor i will form or maintain a tie with j (instead of any other alter).

Assumptions

Similar to TERGM, SAOM is a Markovian model. The network state at each micro-step is assumed to provide all the relevant information necessary to model network change at that moment. In contrast to TERGM, SAOM assumes that network change unfolds in continuous time. In other words, whereas TERGM only considers the shifts between two observable network panels, SAOM considers the *sequencing* of unobserved tie changes. In doing so, SAOM assumes that no two tie changes occur simultaneously; only a single tie can change at any given micro-step. This means that we only violate the assumption of sequential network change when tie changes are exactly simultaneous. In other words, if we were to examine a friendship network, we would be operating under the assumption that no two friendships form in the *exact* same temporal moment. As discussed in Chapter 2, simultaneous tie formation may exist in settings where network ties represent cooperative arrangements. For instance, a network of bilateral trade arrangements or that enforce arms treaties among nations would violate the assumption of sequential change, as multiple ties form simultaneously.

Actors are also assumed to control their outgoing ties but have no control over their incoming ties. Actors are further assumed to pursue the tie changes that align with their preferences, as defined by the researcher. This means that we are implicitly assuming that actors have some knowledge about the complete network structure and other potential alters. As elaborated by Snijders, van de Bunt, and Steglich (2010), this does not imply that actors have exact information about all possible alters or are calculating the exact number of changes to the network that would be realized if a tie were to form. Rather, actors are passingly aware of the network structure and, as such, pursue those tie changes that align with their preferences. The models are referred to as "actor oriented" because ties are assumed to change in accordance with actors' "myopic" pursuit of desirable network positions.

Model Specification

As in TERGM, SAOM can represent structural, dyadic, actor-level, and multiplex effects. These terms are measurements of analogous network statistics presented in Table 2.1 in Chapter 2. The reader will note a key difference between the SAOM representation of network effects and the TERGM representation: Network statistics are defined at the *actor*, rather than *tie*, level. The subscript j for each summation in Table 3.1 reflects this difference. Each statistic is calculated over i's alters to determine the possible changes to the network state that influence the statistics computed on i, rather than the global network statistics computed in TERGM. Hence, coefficients for each network statistic must be interpreted as influencing actors' decisions about which tie to change based on their location in network structure, rather than network structure as a whole. It is in this regard that SAOM provides a *local* interpretation of network effects (the local structures in which actors are embedded influence actors' behavior), whereas TERGM provides a *global* interpretation (changes in the counts of global network statistics influence the probability of a tie changing).

The actor-oriented formulation also highlights a subtle distinction between TERGM and SAOM. Whereas TERGM allows for either between- or within-panel dependencies, SAOM only allows for between-panel dependencies. Actors' decisions are conditional on the current network state and unfold in sequential order. TERGM, by contrast, allows complex substructures to emerge in unison.

SAOM offers the unique ability to specify tie *formation*, *maintenance*, and *withdrawal* as competing processes. The default behavior of RSiena—the most widely used SAOM software package—is to specify all effects as contributing to tie formation and maintenance, where β is the increase/decrease in the log-odds ratio that an actor will form or maintain a tie given a one-unit change in $s(x, y)$. But we can also think of an effect as driving actors to withdraw ties, maintain ties between waves, or create new ties as separate pathways. In practice, researchers are limited in how they can specify each process because of perfect collinearity. It is impossible to specify an effect for all three functions because the processes are a linear combination.

The substantive conclusions reached from each process also usually do not change when distinct pathways are specified. For instance, a negative coefficient for the formation/maintenance function indicates that increases in a network statistic reduce the log-odds that an actor will form or maintain a tie. A positive coefficient for the withdrawal function indicates that increases in a network statistic increase the log-odds that an actor will withdraw a tie. In either scenario, ties are less likely to exist. Because the desired

Term		Formula	Lower-Order Terms
Node matching	●———→●	$\sum_j y_{ij} a_i a_j$	Sender (a), receiver (a)
Node mixing	●———→○	$\sum_j y_{ij} a_i b_j$	Sender (a), receiver (b)
Reciprocation	○←———→○	$\sum_j y_{ij} y_{ji}$	
Reciprocal node matching	●←———→●	$\sum_j y_{ij} y_{ji} a_i a_j$	Sender (a), receiver (a), reciprocity, node matching
Reciprocal node mixing	●←———→○	$\sum_j y_{ij} y_{ji} a_i b_j$	Sender (a,b), receiver (a,b), reciprocity, incoming node mixing, outgoing node mixing
Two-path		$\sum_j y_{ij} y_{jk}$	
Out-two-star		$\sum_j y_{ij} y_{ik}$	
In-2-star		$\sum_j y_{ij} y_{kj}$	
Three-cycle		$\sum_{j,k} y_{ij} y_{jk} y_{ki}$	Two-path
Transitive triplet		$\sum_{j,k} y_{ij} y_{ik} y_{kj}$	Two-path, in-two-star, out-two-star

Table 3.1 Common SAOM terms. y is a tie variable, and a and b are nodal attributes.

interpretation is often available in the default formation/maintenance function, applied researchers typically do not specify competing functions. This is not to say that specifying separate pathways is never useful. As in the case of STERGM, competing pathways may be informative if there is asymmetric causation. But such specifications are uncommon in practice.

Example 3.1. An Actor-Oriented Analysis of Friendship Formation Among Dutch College Students

We can now revisit Van De Bunt's Dutch collegiate friendship network data using SAOM. Here we will specify a similar model as the TERGM in Chapter 2, but in the actor-oriented, rather than tie-oriented, framework. For this example, we will be relying on the RSiena package for R, and we'll model network change as a function of gender, smoking behavior, program length, and endogenous network characteristics.

Data Preparation

Data preparation for SAOM is less intuitive than for TERGM. The most widely used software for SAOM—the RSiena package for R—was originally written as a standalone software package in the early 2000s. When using RSiena, R acts as an interface that sends commands to the standalone SIENA (Simulation Investigation for Empirical Network Analysis) software that estimates the model. Consequently, the interface for RSiena is much more idiosyncratic to the package than statnet or btergm.

The first stages of data preparation for RSiena are similar to btergm. We first arrange our network panel data into a list of sequentially ordered adjacency matrices of identical size. We'll discuss how to modify the assumption of fixed network size later in this chapter. Note also that RSiena assumes that the data are stored as adjacency matrices. Whereas the statnet and btergm packages offer some flexibility in terms of whether the data are stored as an edgelist, adjacency matrix, or network object, RSiena only works with adjacency matrices.

The next thing that we have to do is assign independent variables. RSiena requires that we declare independent variables as Covar objects. RSiena offers two types of covariate objects: time-invariant covariates and time-varying covariates. If the covariate is time invariant, we declare it using the coCovar function (short for constant covariate); if the covariate is time varying, we declare it using the varCovar function (short for varying covariate).

The third step is to wrangle the data by declaring what effects will be included into the model. We first have to arrange the data into a single siena object using the sienaDataCreate function. This function lists the dependent variable and all exogenous covariates that we want to model. After creating the siena object, we next have to specify what network processes we want to model. Our exogenous covariates, for instance, can be specified as sender effects, receiver effects, or interactions, such as homophily or heterophily parameters. We also have to tell RSiena what statistics we want to compute on the endogenously changing network state, such as triads, reciprocity, and degree centrality. The effectsDocumentation function allows us to examine all possible terms for our particular data structure.

Once we have a sense of what we want to include, we tell RSiena to specify the model using the IncludeEffects function. For this example, we'll focus on sender, receiver, and homophily effects for smoking, gender, and program length. As in TERGM, we specify the homophily terms for smoking and gender as matched characteristics and the program length homophily as the absolute difference. We will also include reciprocity, transitive triads, and indegree popularity. However, unlike TERGM, now we include unweighted variants of each statistic—rather than geometrically weighted variants—since SAOM is not affected by degeneracy and interpretation is simpler with unweighted terms.

The final step before estimating the model is to tune the estimation algorithm using the sienaAlgorithmCreate command. This command tells RSiena what parameters—if any—we want to provide to the estimation algorithm to improve convergence, ensure reproducibility, or speed up estimation. For additional details on how to tune the estimation algorithm, please see Ripley, Snijders, Boda, Voros, and Preciado (2020). Once we have the model and algorithm specifications set, we estimate the model using the siena07 command.

Analysis

The SAOM results are presented in column 1 of Table 3.2. The outdegree parameter is analogous to the edges parameter in TERGM. It is the density of each actor's *ego* network, reflecting how many outgoing ties each actor has, on average, when all other terms are at 0. The negative coefficient for outdegree indicates that the probability of i choosing to nominate a random actor as a friend when all covariates are at 0 is small. The receiver effect for gender is an *alter* effect; it means that the odds that a student will nominate another student as a friend are 32% higher ($exp(.21) = 1.32$) if the other student is female, as opposed to male. The sender effect is .39, indicating that female students have 48% higher odds ($exp(.39) = 1.48$) of nominating another student as a friend (send an outgoing tie) as compared to male students. The homophily effect is nonsignificant for gender.

Turning to smoking effects, the receiver effect is negative. This means that the sampled Dutch students are less likely to nominate other students as friends if the other student is a nonsmoker. Alternatively, the sender effect is positive, meaning that nonsmokers tend to nominate more friends than smokers. The smoking homophily coefficient is nonsignificant.

	1. MoM estimates (seed = 21093)	2. MoM estimates (seed = 21092)[b]
Outdegree	−2.16*** (.500)	−2.08*** (.439)
Female		
Receiver	.21* (.092)	.21* (.097)
Sender	.39** (.101)	.40** (.096)
Same	.05 (.075)	.06 (.072)
Nonsmoker		
Receiver	−.18** (.064)	−.18* (.068)
Sender	.84*** (.083)	.84*** (.081)
Same	.01 (.057)	.01 (.058)
Program length		
Receiver	−.09* (.047)	−.09* (.046)
Sender	.41*** (.056)	.41*** (.053)
Absolute difference	−.12** (.044)	−.12* (.041)
Reciprocity	.71*** (.069)	.71*** (.07)
Transitive triad	1.49* (.666)	1.38* (.592)
Indegree popularity	.04* (.013)	.04* (.013)

Table 3.2 SAOM of the Van De Bunt network.[a] Coefficients and standard errors reported for all models.

Note: The seed is the numeric random value used to initiate the stochastic approximation algorithm used to approximate the MoM estimator. MoM = method of moments.
[a] Rate parameters are omitted from tables.
[b] Reestimate of column 1 with different starting seed for stochastic approximation.
*$p < .05$. **$p < .01$. ***$p < .001$.

The default behavior of RSiena is to center all variables on their means, so we have to take centering into account when we interpret coefficients for continuous variables.[2] The program length receiver effect is −.09, meaning that the odds that a student will nominate another student as a friend decrease by 9% ($exp(−.09) = .913$) when alters' program length is 1 year above the mean program length. The program length sender effect is .41, meaning that the odds that a focal actor will form an outgoing tie with another student increases by 51% ($exp(.41) = 1.51$) when the focal student is 1 year above the mean program length. The absolute difference in program length

---

[2] Technically, binary variables are centered as well, but centering has no influence on the interpretation of binary effects because the spacing between each group is still 1 for all group members.

coefficient is significant and negative, indicating that students are more likely to form ties with one another when they are in programs of a similar length.

Because the endogenous network statistics are calculated at the actor level, they are interpreted differently in SAOM than in TERGM. The key here is that the interpretation focuses on *actors'* decisions, as opposed to the probability of realizing a tie. The reciprocity statistic has the most similar interpretation. The positive coefficient for reciprocity indicates that i is more likely to nominate j as a friend if j already considers i a friend. Here, the odds that i will nominate j as a friend double if j has already nominated i as a friend in the past ($exp(.71) = 2.01$).

The transitive triad statistic tells us that i is more likely to form an outgoing friendship with j if i and j both perceive k to be a friend. The coefficient for transitive triads is 1.49, reflecting a preference for triadic closure. Students have 4.4 times higher odds ($exp(1.49) = 4.43$) of nominating another student as a friend if the outgoing tie closes a transitive triplet.

Indegree popularity tells us whether increases in popularity (increases in indegree) make students more likely to befriend other students (send outgoing ties). The indegree popularity parameter is .04, reflecting a tendency for students who have received a large number of friendship nominations to initiate a greater number of outgoing friendship ties. Each unit increase in indegree popularity increases the odds that a focal student will nominate another student as a friend by 4% ($exp(.04) = 1.04$).

Model Checking

We estimated the model in column 1 using method of moments. In practice, a stochastic approximation algorithm is standard for approximating the moment estimator in SAOM. This algorithmic approach uses a large number of simulations to find reasonable parameter estimates. If we were to attempt to calculate every possible network change process for the network, we would encounter similar levels of computational expensiveness that we observed in TERGM. Stochastic approximation speeds up this process by randomly exploring a number of plausible network change processes and pooling the coefficients from those simulations. Thus, the first thing we need to do when model checking is ensure that the approximation algorithm has converged. If the algorithm has not converged, that means that our simulated network change processes have not yielded a stable set of coefficients, and therefore our modeling results are uninterpretable.

For each parameter, siena07 returns a t-convergence ratio. These t ratios are used to evaluate whether our particular coefficients yield stable estimates across simulation trials, where smaller values indicate more stability.

A value between $-.1$ and 1 reflects good convergence, while larger absolute values indicate that the parameter estimates are unstable. A t-convergence ratio is also returned for the model as a whole. Here, we ideally observe a t-convergence ratio below $.25$. If all parameter t ratios have an absolute value lower than $.1$ and a model t ratio lower than $.25$, we can conclude that the algorithm has converged. In our SAOM, all parameter t ratios are between $-.1$ and $.1$, and the model t ratio is $.14$. We can therefore conclude that the estimation algorithm has converged.

If either criterion is poor, we can improve convergence by updating the model. This involves reestimating the SAOM but using the coefficients from our previous (failed) estimation attempt as starting values. In large networks or complicated models, it is common to update the model multiple times to achieve good convergence. The prevAns parameter in the siena07 function provides functionality for initiating SAOM estimates with coefficients from an earlier model. We can also help convergence by increasing the number of simulations in the stochastic approximation algorithm in the call to sienaAlgorithmCreate (see Chapter 3 Supplementary Code for examples).

Goodness of fit is evaluated by simulating network statistics from the model and comparing the statistics to the observed network statistics. The underlying logic here is similar to TERGM: If our model is doing a good job of representing the data, then any simulated networks derived from our model should be reasonable representations of the data. We can assess this by simulating a distribution of network statistics—indegree, outdegree, triad census—and comparing their distributions to our data.

Figure 3.1 plots goodness-of-fit results. The solid line measures the statistics of the observed network, while the violin plots represent the interquartile range for the simulated network statistics. The indegree distribution is a strong fit with no significant difference between the simulated networks and the observed networks. The triad census is also recaptured fairly well for most types of triads, despite a statistically significant p value. However, the outdegree distribution is poorly represented in the model. This suggests that model fit could potentially be improved by including terms that better represent the outdegree distribution, such as specifications that allow for a nonuniform rate function across actors. This is straightforward to specify by including the outRate parameter in the includeEffects function, which allows ρ_i to vary as a function of actors' outdegree.

Improvements in model fit are evaluated using the score-type tests proposed by Schweinberger (2012). The score-type tests are implemented in the score.Test function in RSiena. The test evaluates whether the difference between the simulated and observed network statistics is significantly increased when the specified parameter(s) are excluded from the model.

54

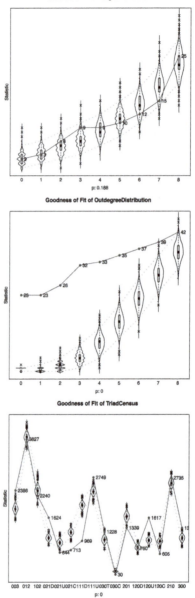

Figure 3.1 Goodness of fit for SAOM. Violin plots report interquartile range for simulated statistics of target network (here, Wave 7 Van De Bunt network). Solid line traces observed statistics of the target network. The *p* value tests the null hypothesis that the simulated and observed distributions are equal.

A significant result means that including the tested parameter(s) improves model fit.

We can apply the score-type tests to evaluate the importance of homophily effects. Even though the coefficients for gender homophily and smoking homophily are nonsignificant, it is possible that including both parameters jointly improves model performance. In this case, the joint score-type test for gender and smoking homophily is nonsignificant ($\chi^2 = .58, p = .75$), indicating that jointly including the two homophily parameters does not significantly improve model performance. We can therefore safely exclude both covariates from our model.

A final diagnostic is collinearity. Because SAOM does not rely on convergence to a stationary MCMC distribution, the consequences of collinearity for SAOM are less severe than in TERGM. Collinearity can, however, lead to instability in SAOM standard errors, where multiple reruns of the same model lead to different variance estimates. The simplest way to check this is to examine the correlation matrix, where correlations larger than .9 may be evidence of a collinearity issue. However, if standard errors are stable when reestimating the model, then there is little cause for concern even when correlations are large. In the SAOM above, the transitive triad and indegree popularity parameters are correlated at .92. But reestimating the model with another starting seed value does little to change the estimated parameter values and standard errors (column 2, Table 3.2). It is therefore reasonable to conclude that collinearity is not problematizing SAOM results.

Missing Data

Much like the btergm package, the default behavior in RSiena is to handle missing data among independent variables by imputing the mean for nodal covariates. Alternative values, such as the median or mode, can also be imputed using the imputationValues argument available within coCovar and varCovar. For network variables, missing data are handled by carrying forward the most recently observed tie value. If two actors are connected in the first panel, but data are missing for the second panel, then a value of "1" would be imputed indicating that the actors are assumed to be connected in the second panel. Missing ties in the first panel are treated as "0." SAOM estimates using these procedures tend to be fairly robust to modest amounts of missing data (Hipp et al., 2015; Huisman & Steglich, 2008).

When there is more than roughly 20% missing data, more sophisticated imputation procedures are necessary. Krause, Huisman, and Snijders (2018) expand standard multiple imputation frameworks that allow researchers to generate multiple data sets and to pool them under the assumption that data are missing at random. For exogenous attributes, no special procedures are necessary, and the method of Krause, Huisman, and Snijders (2018) reduces to conventional multiple imputation (Rubin, 1976).

For missing tie data, Krause, Huisman, and Snijders (2018) propose to use model-based imputation to impute missing data. The logic behind this strategy is similar to multiple imputation in classical regression. In standard multiple imputation, we leverage covariance between variables to provide estimates of missing values. We then pool estimates from multiple imputations to smooth over any error in our imputations. In the model-based imputation approach, we formulate a model that we think is reasonable for the data and use the predictions from that model to create several imputed data sets and then pool the estimates from models fit to those data sets.

First, we specify an ERGM or use the Bayesian ERGM augmentation strategy of Koskinen et al. (2013) to impute missing data on the first network panel. Next, we use the imputed Wave 1 network to fit a SAOM predicting change between the imputed Wave 1 network and unimputed Wave 2 network. We then use the estimated coefficients to predict the missing data. We reiterate this process in a sequential fashion until we have imputed missing data for each network panel. As in standard multiple imputation, we typically repeat this process 5 to 10 times to obtain a range of possible data structures resulting from the imputation procedures. We then fit a SAOM to each of the simulated data sets and finally pool the estimates for interpretation.

Advanced Interpretation

Like TERGM (Duxbury, 2021c), SAOM coefficients cannot be compared between models or groups. This is because of SAOM's reliance on multinomial logistic regression to estimate the model.[3] However, marginal effects are a less elegant solution in the context of SAOM as compared to TERGM. A peculiar property of multinomial logistic regression is that the average marginal effect can provide the opposite sign and different levels of significance as compared to the coefficient (Wiersema & Bowen, 2009). Hence, we may get contradictory results if we interpret the marginal effect instead of the coefficient in SAOM.

One solution to this issue that has received increasing attention in recent studies is the use of predicted values (Schaefer & Kreager, 2020; Snijders & Lomi, 2019). In this framework, we hold all controls at their mean and

---

[3]The coefficients of a multinomial logistic regression absorb the variance of omitted variables, even when they are uncorrelated with measured variables. As a consequence, the coefficients are only unbiased when we are certain there are no omitted variables—an untestable assumption.

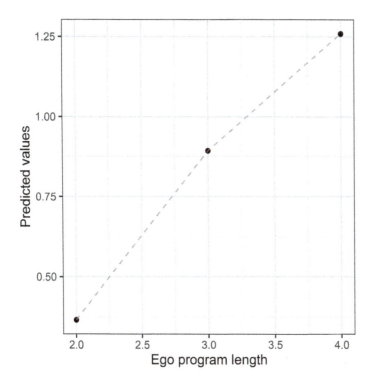

Figure 3.2 Predicted values for program length when alter program
length is held at its mean and all other covariates are held at 0.
Estimates based on SAOM in column 1 of Table 3.2.

predict the probability that a tie will form at as a function of the variables
of interest. If the predicted values are significantly greater for one group
than another, we can conclude that moderation exists. If the predicted values
change by a large amount between models, we can conclude confounding.

Figure 3.2 depicts the predicted values of a tie forming as the absolute
difference in program length increases when holding alter program length
at the mean (3.36). The results illustrate that the log-odds that a student
will befriend another increases as ego program length increases. Notably,
there is a marginal decrease in the effect of ego program length when the
absolute difference between ego and alter increases as ego program length
moves from 3 to 4. This result is consistent with our primary results for the

absolute difference parameter, indicating that actors tend to prefer actors of similar program length. In other words, the results in Figure 3.2 indicate that two students are most likely to become friends when they are in the program for a similar amount of time.

We can also evaluate the significance of interactions using score-type tests. The logic of this strategy mirrors the likelihood-ratio test strategy proposed by Allison (1999) for logistic regression, where moderation is evaluated by using model fit criteria instead of the significance of the parameter, which may be biased. For our example, the single parameter score-type test of the absolute difference parameter is significant ($\chi^2 = 7.33, p = .007$), supporting the significance of the interaction.

Another quirk of SAOM regards asymptotic inference. At first blush, the idea of generalizing to a population and associated concepts of statistical power are unclear in SAOM (Stadfeld, Snijders, Steglich, & van Duijn, 2020), since the data used to formulate the model are themselves simulated. However, these issues are clarified if we recall the *process-oriented* interpretation of parameters discussed in Chapter 2. We can regard SAOM p values as representing that probability that the true coefficient that generated our data is 0 given that we estimated a particular coefficient from our sample. If we get a small p value, this implies that we are unlikely to observe a coefficient this large and have the true relationship equal 0. In this sense, the p value can be thought of as representing the probability that we should observe similar determinants of network change if we were to sample a comparable set of actors from a comparable social network. Snijders (2001) shows through simulation that the critical values obtained from SAOM approximate Student's t-distribution, and so p values are more interpretable than in the case of TERGM.

Note here that the process-oriented interpretation relies on the appropriateness of SAOM assumptions for the data. If the assumptions of sequential, agent-driven change are untenable, then our model misrepresents the data-generating process, and consequently, any assessments of statistical significance and effect sizes are uninformative. Put differently, we cannot generalize to a true generative process if our model fundamentally misrepresents that process. We must therefore direct careful consideration to the assumption of agent-driven change and sequential ordering of tie changes before deciding on SAOM for our analysis.

Other Modeling Considerations

Joiners and Leavers

SAOM assumes that network size is constant across repeated measurements. This assumption is often violated. Actors may enter or leave a network, for instance, when high school students drop out or graduate. One strategy for dealing with this issue is the method of "joiners and leavers" proposed by Huisman and Snijders (2003). The method extends the simulation algorithm used in the imputation stage by allowing actors to join or leave the network at each micro-step but also tends to increase estimation times. An often preferred method is to control for varying network composition by including an offset matrix into the model. The matrix contains structural 0s for all dyads that are active on the network at a time period and values of 1 for all dyads including actors who are absent during the time period. The offset matrix essentially "fixes effects" by controlling for all possible ties to actors who are not present on the network.

Big Networks

A second modeling consideration is scalability. SAOM was designed with moderately sized networks in mind, as actors are assumed to have knowledge of the total network structure (Snijders, 2001, p. 373). In large networks, actors are unlikely to have global knowledge of the network structure, and there is a large degree of internal heterogeneity among actors' motivations. Some isolated applications suggest that model fit suffers in large network data (Lewis & Kaufman, 2018). A strategy to help handle heterogeneity in large network data is to specify local risk sets. If the set of possible alters is identifiable, say through a community detection algorithm or prespecified nesting structure, it is possible to include a time-varying offset matrix with 0s for possible alters and 1s for dyads where ties are impossible. For instance, if we analyze students nested in different schools, we first combine all school networks into a single block matrix. We then create an offset matrix with 1s for cross-school ties and 0s otherwise. Finally, we include the offset matrix as a covariate in our model, treating the pooled block matrix of school networks as the dependent variable. See Turanovic and Young (2016) or Schaefer (2018) for applied examples.

An additional benefit of specifying local risk sets is that it helps to reduce estimation times. Beyond problems with internal heterogeneity, large networks often present convergence problems for SAOM because of the complexity of finding reasonable network change processes and parameters for those change processes. If we are able to parse the network into distinct subgraphs, then we can take a "divide-and-conquer" approach to model fitting by estimating a unique SAOM for each subgraph and pooling the results for final presentation.

Time Heterogeneity

A third modeling consideration is time heterogeneity. SAOM assumes that effects are homogeneous across time periods. If we expect that girls in high school friendship networks are more social than boys, this assumption states that the effect of gender should be the same at each panel observation. This assumption can be violated when the coefficient for gender—or any variable of interest—is correlated with the passage of time or interacts with the passage of time. In these cases, we say there is "unobserved" time heterogeneity, referring to temporal variation that is not included in the model. The consequences of unobserved time heterogeneity are comparable to standard omitted variable bias: It may cause standard errors and coefficients to be inaccurate.

We can implement several procedures for testing and accounting for time heterogeneity. These procedures involve including dummy variables for each network panel into our model using the includeTimeDummy function in RSiena and testing for improvements in model fit. In the Van De Bunt friendship network, for instance, we observe the network over seven time periods, so it is likely that there is some heterogeneity between time periods. We can use Schweinberger's (2012) score-type tests to evaluate differences in parameters between time periods with the sienaTimeTest function. A joint test of time heterogeneity for the entire model indicates significant time heterogeneity ($\chi^2 = 284.36, p < .001$). This means that there are period effects in our data, where more tie changes occur in between some network panels as compared to others. To address this, we would retain the time dummy variables in our model to account for period effects.

While our first evaluation considered unmeasured period effects, it may also be the case that a variable *interacts* with time. The sienaTimeTest function evaluates this possibility by including interactions between each variable and the time dummy variables. A significant score-type test for any parameter tells us that the parameter varies across time, and thus there is time heterogeneity for that parameter. The results from these tests are presented in column 1 of Table 3.3. With the exception of gender sender and receiver effects and the smoking receiver effect, there is significant time heterogeneity for every parameter.

When unobserved time heterogeneity is uncovered for a specific parameter, we typically address the issue by including an interaction between that

	1. p value	2. p value[a]
Outdegree	.000	NA
Female		
Receiver	.245	.265
Sender	.434	.324
Same	.000	.143
Nonsmoker		
Receiver	.679	.130
Sender	.000	.000
Same	.000	.001
Program length		
Receiver	.130	.136
Sender	.000	.000
Absolute difference	.000	.672
Reciprocity	.000	.000
Transitive triad	.000	.794
Indegree popularity	.000	.005

Table 3.3 The p values from two-tailed tests of time heterogeneity in Van De Bunt network SAOM parameters.

[a]Model with time dummies included. Outdegree parameter is missing because time dummies specify separate outdegree parameters for each panel.

parameter and the time period, allowing the coefficient to vary across time. As suggested above, we need to be careful in balancing the desire to correct time heterogeneity against maintaining a parsimonious model. It is sometimes the case that we can control for parameter-specific time heterogeneity without including an interaction between that parameter and time. This tends to occur when a specific coefficient, say gender, correlates with an unmeasured period effect.

To make this possibility more concrete, we'll reevaluate the results in column 1 of Table 3.3. Here our parameter-specific tests are compared to a reference model that does not include the time dummy variable main effects. It is therefore possible that each interaction is significant simply because there is an unmeasured period effect and that unmeasured period effect correlates with many of our parameters. If this is true, then we may be able to reduce the parameter-specific time heterogeneity by controlling for unmeasured period effects. Column 2 of Table 3.3 reports results for time heterogeneity tests that consider this possibility by including time dummy variables in the primary SAOM and then reestimating the time heterogeneity tests. Although time heterogeneity still persists in the model at large (joint test: $\chi^2 = 189.61, p < .001$), it is reduced substantially for most parameters. Column 2 of Table 3.3 shows that there is no longer significant time heterogeneity for the gender homophily parameter, program length homophily parameter, or the transitive triad parameter. In this case, we were able to reduce the severity of our time heterogeneity problem for specific parameters without including interactions with time.

Table 3.4 reports results from SAOM that includes time dummy variables. Estimates are mostly consistent after correcting for time heterogeneity. Including controls for time, however, does influence some conclusions about coefficient size and significance. The sender and receiver effects for gender as well as the sender effect for smoking and program length both substantially increase in size after including controls for the time period.

	1. Controls for Time Heterogeneity[b]
Outdegree	−2.13* (.913)
Female	
Receiver	.32* (.132)
Sender	.66** (.171)
Same	.04 (.025)
Nonsmoker	
Receiver	−.09 (.078)
Sender	1.30*** (.188)
Same	−.003 (.066)
Program length	
Receiver	−.03 (.055)
Sender	.70*** (.125)
Absolute difference	−.132** (.048)
Reciprocity	.75*** (.081)
Transitive triad	1.79 (1.31)
Indegree popularity	.03 (.025)

Table 3.4   Time heterogeneity SAOM of the Van De Bunt network.[a] Coefficients and standard errors reported. Models estimated using method of moments.

[a]Rate parameters are omitted from the table.
[b]Time dummy variables included.
*$p < .05$. **$p < .01$. ***$p < .001$.

Alternatively, the coefficients for the smoking receiver effect, indegree pop-ularity, and transitive triad parameters are now nonsignificant.

Sample Constraints

Finally, as in TERGM, the model may not reflect constraints on the network sample, such as when outgoing ties are limited during data collection. Recall from Chapter 2 that this often occurs during survey administration, where respondents are limited in the number of alters they are able to nominate. We can place constraints on the number of outgoing ties by specifying the MaxDegree parameter in sienaAlgorithmCreate to adjust our estimates to reflect the maximum possible number of outgoing ties.

Model Extensions

The actor-based formulation of SAOM lends itself to a number of exten-sions. In Chapter 5, for instance, we will consider extensions to behavioral data. SAOM can also be used for multivariate network analysis. Snijders et al. (2013) introduce a model for the *coevolution* of multiple networks that provides actors with the opportunity to update network ties in two sepa-rate networks. This multivariate formulation allows researchers to move past multiplexity to examine how the *structure* of one network can contribute to tie formation in another network. SAOM has also been extended to bipartite (Snijders et al., 2013) and multilevel (An, 2015b) networks. And the multi-variate network model can be used to examine the coevolution of unipartite and bipartite networks.

An additional utility of SAOM is that it lends itself to agent-based simu-lation (Snijders & Steglich, 2015). For instance, adams and Schaefer (2016) examine how network interventions might be leveraged to reduce adolescent smoking behavior by manipulating the structure of an AddHealth friendship network and then using SAOM to simulate how smoking behavior devel-ops on the manipulated network structure. A colleague of mine and myself used a similar research design to evaluate how various network-based polic-ing strategies affect drug trafficking on darknet drug markets (Duxbury & Haynie, 2020a).

Selecting a Network Panel Model

The decision about whether to use SAOM or TERGM in applied settings is nontrivial. From afar, TERGM and SAOM look quite similar. There is an interesting degree of correspondence between the two models. Snijders (2001), for instance, showed through simulation that, if allowed to reach equilibrium, the SAOM simulation procedure generates an ERG distribution, implying that SAOM is conditionally equivalent to ERGM at the stationary distribution. Both models can also be regarded as arising from a random utility model. For SAOM, this is because actors' tie change decisions are formulated as an outcome of discrete choice (Pink, Kretschmer, & Leszczensky, 2020). For TERGM, this is because the observed ties can be regarded as a binary realization of a latent utility function (Duxbury, 2021c).

Despite their theoretical similarities, SAOM and TERGM tell us different things about the network change process. Block et al. (2019), for instance, show that the models can provide different conclusions when applied to the same data. Comparing the first columns in Tables 2.2 and 3.2, we see some concurrence and some divergence. In TERGM, for instance, the female sender effect is insignificant, while in SAOM, it is significant. The magnitude of the effects also differs substantially. In SAOM, the sender effect of gender is larger than the receiver effect, while in TERGM, the coefficient for the receiver effect is far larger. If our primary interest is in interpreting how gender influences outgoing ties, SAOM and TERGM would lead us to reach different conclusions on the importance of gender for friendships.

So, which model should you use? Empirical assessments have yet to provide a clear conclusion on the superiority of one model over the other. On the grounds of out-of-sample predictions, for instance, neither TERGM nor SAOM are particularly accurate (Block et al., 2018; Leifeld & Cranmer, 2019). There is also currently debate about the criteria upon which models should be evaluated and whether analysts should prioritize prediction or explanation when adjudicating between models.

One consideration that should inform model selection is whether an actor-oriented framework is appropriate for the data. Schaefer and Marcum (2017) argue that TERGM and SAOM answer different research questions. While TERGM tells us whether network structures emerge between waves, SAOM tells us how actors pursue network states that align with their preferences. For studies where the network change process is strictly an outcome of agent-driven behavior, SAOM is likely preferable. In the case of economic relations, for instance, ties will never arise without actors pursuing those connections. TERGM makes less sense in this context, as it seems unrealistic to regard the structure of economic relations as the outcome of a global network process.

Alternatively, if we are modeling change in sociotechnological networks, like the World Wide Web (Albert, Jeong, & Barabasi, 1999), it makes little sense to regard the network as comprising purposively driven agents. In many cases, it may not be clear whether the assumption of agent-driven change is reasonable. In the case of friendship networks, students certainly choose their friends, but their choice behavior is subject to constraints. For instance, students are probably more likely to form friends with alters who have the same homeroom or are on the same sports team. In this instance, friendships are informed as much by contextual constraints as deliberate choice behavior. SAOM is perfectly capable of modeling such constraints, but in practice, these types of constraints are less frequently included in empirical studies. This is an important omission in current SAOM applications. For SAOM estimates to be informative when the assumption of agent-driven change is only true under limiting conditions, constraints on agent behavior are as important to include as factors that motivate agents' choices.

A second consideration regards the timing of network change. TERGM regards network structures as emergent *ex nihilo*, while SAOM asserts order onto the unmeasured change process. Figure 3.3, for instance, depicts triadic closure in two network panels. TERGM would regard the entire triad structure as emerging from an empty triad in one unobserved moment. SAOM would impute the unmeasured change sequence by assuming purposeful agent behavior. There is no clear-cut answer on which treatment should be preferred. The expectation that structure forms "from nothing" is unrealistic in many research settings. But the assumption that actors drive the sequencing of network change in pursuit of their preferences may also be unpalatable.

While the considerations above emphasize theoretical reasoning, there is some evidence that TERGM performs worse when there are large time periods between panel observations (Block et al., 2018). It is more likely that tie changes will go unobserved when there are long time periods between panels (e.g., if an *ij* tie dissolves and then forms again). It is also less likely that the network panels will reflect the network structure at the time of a tie change. If the network panel data are collected at long time intervals, SAOM may be preferred.

Practical Guidance

The following recommendations should help practitioners select an appropriate model. The first question a researcher should ask themselves is, "Does agent-driven change make sense for my data?" If the answer is "no," then

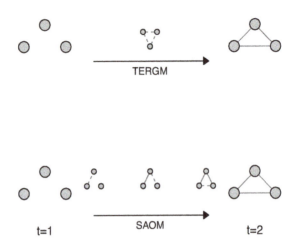

Figure 3.3   Treatment of unobserved change in SAOM and TERGM

SAOM is not a valid modeling strategy. All statistical evidence arising from SAOM depends on the appropriateness of this assumption. Regardless of any weaknesses of TERGM, SAOM results are uninterpretable if the assumption of agent-driven change cannot be met. Similarly, SAOM results are uninformative if we are examining a network where ties often form in unison in discrete moments in time (i.e., tie changes are not sequentially ordered), such as bilateral trade arrangements.

The second question a researcher should ask regards the theoretical process of interest. Do researchers only expect between-panel dependencies, or do they also expect within-panel dependencies? If the answer is the former, then either SAOM or TERGM will work. If the answer is the latter, SAOM cannot address the research question or bring evidence to bear on the within-panel dependencies of interest.

Third, researchers should ask, How much time has passed between observations? If several years have passed between observations, then the TERGM assumption that the order of unobserved tie changes is inconsequential will probably be unreasonable. In this case, SAOM should be preferred as long as other modeling assumptions are met. Fourth, researchers should consider whether the sequencing of ties is theoretically important. If we are examining a network where there is a lot of tie activity in a short time window, then SAOM will be preferable even if repeated measurements are taken with a good amount of granularity.

The final consideration bears on interpretation. Are researchers interested in a tie-based or an agent-based interpretation of model output? Put differently, is their theoretical argument one about individuals' choice behavior or one about the distribution of relationships? If researchers are interested in interpreting how local network effects influence individual behavior, SAOM makes more sense. Although TERGM can be formulated to provide an actor-level interpretation, it is not explicitly factored into the modeling framework, nor are local network effects. Alternatively, if researchers are interested in the distribution of ties, are not exclusively interested in an agent-level interpretation, or their theoretical model implies a *global* as opposed to local network process, TERGM will provide an interpretation that bears more directly on the research question.

Conclusion

Decisions about the suitability of SAOM and TERGM should be made with respect to a given research question. In observational network panel data, for instance, continuous time often makes sense. In experimental settings, on the other hand, network dynamics are structured as discrete occurrences (Centola, 2010; Melamed, Harrell, & Simpson, 2018). In these circumstances, it makes less sense to impose a continuous time model on the analysis when, by design, tie changes are discrete. Further, as we will discuss in the next chapter, sometimes discrete timing is sufficient to draw substantive conclusions, as the exact timing of tie changes is less relevant than their approximate order.

For further reading, a nontechnical discussion of SAOM can be found in Snijders, van de Bunt, and Steglich (2010). For a technical overview, researchers should consult Snijders (2017). Detailed guidelines on the nuances of the RSiena software package are available in Ripley et al. (2020). Applied examples of SAOM can be found in Schaefer et al. (2011); Lewis and Kaufman (2018); Duxbury and Haynie (2020b); Turanovic and Young (2016); Block (2015); Ragan et al. (2014); Haynie, Doogan, and Soller (2014); or Schaefer and Kreager (2020).

CHAPTER 4. MODELING RELATIONAL EVENT DATA

Network panel data provide a series of snapshots of a network at distinct moments in time. The data on timing are coarse. We do not know exactly when ties changed, although we can re-create the scope of network change by comparing two panel observations. But what if we know the exact moment of tie changes? We may have data on the minute or second that an email is sent, the exact duration of a phone call, or how much time two friends spent together at the bar. How should we handle such ties?

Historically, scholars would typically deal with such data structures by aggregating information over multiple time periods (Butts, 2009; Kitts, 2014). The researcher would make a theoretically informed decision on what snapshot offered the most accurate network representation. For example, we might combine email communications into 12 individual month-long observation windows to represent a year of email activity. Then, the researcher would apply a network panel model to examine how the network evolved.

We can get a lot of mileage out of this approach. But it also presents unique problems. First and foremost, both TERGM and SAOM assume that ties persist across time periods unless altered. If we were to fit a SAOM to the hypothetical 12-period email communication network, for instance, our model would assume that an email communication only disappeared if an actor chose to terminate that communication. Obviously, this is not how emails work. The communication has its own short-lived time frame that terminates once an email is sent. Thus, we need a model that assumes that ties only exist within well-defined, typically short-lived observation windows.

The second problem relates to the sequencing of network ties. With network panel data, we have limited information on the order in which ties changed. Consequently, network panel models make assumptions to deal with the sequencing of unobserved ties. With relational event data, that sequencing is available. We would therefore prefer a model that makes use of this rich information.

The third problem relates to waiting periods. When looking at *event* data, such as the timing of mortality, policy changes, or pregnancy, we are often substantively interested in the *time* to event occurrence. With relational event data, questions of timing and duration are also prevalent. Many ties may be activated in a short time window followed by periods of relative silence. We may want to know what network structures decrease the time between social interactions in organizational settings or economic exchanges between market actors. In these cases, aggregating the data into distinct snapshots discards important information on the timing of event activity.

These three considerations are at the heart of relational event models (REM) (Butts, 2008). REM is inspired by modeling strategies familiar to sequence analysis and event history analysis. REM models the *sequencing* of tie changes as a function of endogenous network effects and exogenous time-invariant and time-varying node attributes. In this respect, the model takes seriously the order in which relational events occur. Further, the model explicitly accounts for the waiting period between events, allowing researchers to interpret coefficients as affecting the *time* to event occurrence. And, in contrast to network panel models, REM assumes that ties form and dissolve within discrete time windows, rather than persisting across observation periods.

What Are Relational Event Data?

There are two key distinctions between relational event data and network panel data. The first regards timing. In relational event data, we know exactly when a tie emerges, how long it exists, and when it dissipates. The second distinction regards the *nature* of a tie. Relational events are exactly that: *events* that occur between actors. Relational events can be thought of as mutual occurrences connecting at least two actors. Golf games, beer drinking sessions, romantic encounters, television viewing parties, phone calls, and business meetings can all be viewed as relational events. Each observation is a discrete event occurring in continuous time.

The Relational Event Model (REM)

The analysis of relational events is one of *hazard* rates (Butts, 2008; Perry & Wolfe, 2013). We model how frequently events are activated within specific time frames and what are the determinants of event reactivation over repeated observations. This was Butts's (2008) premise when he developed the relational event model (REM). REM regards the analysis of relational event data as one of event timing and frequency.

We can regard observed relational events as the outcome of a stochastic process, where multiple actors are "at risk" of participating in a relational event but are constrained by the characteristics of a time-varying network. These two processes are in display in Figure 4.1. The first component is the event activity at each observation. Actors form connections that disappear at the end of each observation window. The second component is

70

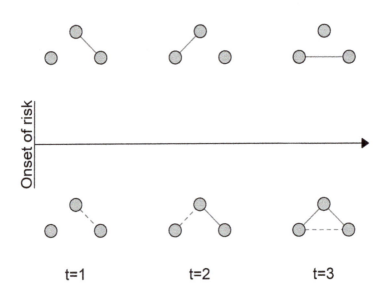

Figure 4.1 Example of relational event data. Top panel is the event activity at each observation, and bottom panel is the network structure of prior relational events.

network structure. The observed network accrues from prior relational events, forming a structure in which each actor is embedded. Thus, although relational events only occupy discrete moments in time, the cumulative network structure of *prior* events may impact which events are activated next in the sequence of relational events.

To formulate this model mathematically, we express the probability of observing a number of events at a given time period out of all possible events that *could* have been observed at the same time period. Let the number of events at a given time period be represented by $n_{ij}(t)$ and $\lambda_{ij}(t)$ be the hazard rate. The model giving us the probability that a specific number of ties connect a focal dyad within a specific time period is

$$Pr(n_{ij}(t)) = \frac{\lambda_{ij}(t)^{n_{ij}(t)} \cdot exp(-\lambda_{ij}(t))}{n_{ij}(t)!}. \quad (4.1)$$

We assume an inhomogeneous local Poisson process, meaning that the event rates at each time period are assumed to be Poisson distributed with nonconstant hazard rates across the time periods.

To formulate the probability model in Equation 4.2, we have to know not only which actors engaged in a relational event but also which dyads *could* have engaged in an event but did not. In most applications, the risk set—all dyads that could possibly engage in an event—is defined by all actors who have been connected at some point in the event sequence. Actors first appear once they have engaged in an event and remain at risk from then on. This definition of the risk set is flexible and can be altered depending on the empirical context (see, e.g., Brandenberger, 2018).

In practice, we are concerned with analyzing the factors that increase or decrease the hazard rate. This gives us a generalized linear model for the hazard rate:

$$\lambda_{ij}(t) = exp(\lambda_0 + \theta^T z(x, Y)). \tag{4.2}$$

Here, x is a set of exogenous covariates provided by the researcher. These may include characteristics for the actor who initiates a relational event or characteristics for the actor who receives a relational event. Y represents the network of prior relational events, or the "event sequence" in the language of Butts (2008). $z(.)$ is a mapping function that calculates statistics on the exogenous characteristics and on the network of earlier events. λ_0 is the baseline hazard rate, and θ is the parameter vector to be estimated from our data. We can interpret θ as the increase or decrease in the log-hazard rate corresponding to a one-unit increase in $z(x, Y)$.

The Intuition

The model in Equations 4.1 and 4.2 may look intimidating. But we can simplify it greatly by conceptualizing REM as containing two stages: data preparation and estimation. In the preparation stage, we transform our network data into a relational event data set, including observations for the at-risk dyads. This process involves taking an edgelist and including observations for the events that *did not* occur but could have. Once we have constructed the risk set, we get a data matrix that looks something like this:

$$
\begin{bmatrix}
Sender & Receiver & Time & Event \\
1 & 2 & 1 & 0 \\
1 & 3 & 1 & 0 \\
2 & 1 & 1 & 0 \\
2 & 3 & 1 & 1 \\
3 & 1 & 1 & 1 \\
3 & 2 & 1 & 0 \\
1 & 2 & 2 & 1 \\
\vdots & \vdots & \vdots & \vdots \\
i & j & t & --
\end{bmatrix}
$$

The expanded risk set is identical to an edgelist but now includes all observations where an event *could* have occurred. The sender column records the actor who initiates a relational event, the receiver column records the actor who receives an event, and the event column tells us whether an event occurred. This representation clarifies the relationship between REM and sequence analysis. By sorting the events according to their temporal order, we are able to reconstruct the exact sequencing of tie changes and the network structures that existed at the moment of each tie change.

In the estimation stage, we fit a regression to the preprocessed data, treating the event indicator variable as the dependent variable. In this stage, REM reduces to a standard event history model. This is because the preprocessed data are conditionally independent and therefore can be analyzed using standard regression frameworks. If our timing data are exact (e.g., available at the day, minute, or second), we estimate the REM as a Cox proportional hazard model. If our timing is not exact but we know the order of events, we can estimate the REM as a discrete time model by fitting a logistic regression to the preprocessed data.

Thus, we can think of REM as a Cox model or logistic regression for the long-formatted survival data. The two key differences between REM and a standard survival analysis are that the unit of analysis is the dyad-time period and we are able to include network statistics on the right-hand side of our equation.

Assumptions

A key assumption in REM is that each event is associated with a single time point. This means that if the same dyad is connected at two consecutive time periods, we regard this tie as being *repeated* at the second observation, rather than *persisting* between observations.

REM also assumes that events are uninfluenced by *nonoccurring* events. In other words, the fact that an event *did not* occur should have no influence over the events that do occur. As an example, say that we are examining the frequency of phone calls between two friends, Sally and Jane. Imagine that we measure a phone call between Sally and Jane on Monday and that the two friends chat again on Wednesday. REM would assume that the *absence* of a phone conversation on Tuesday is irrelevant for modeling the phone call on Wednesday. The implicit assumption in this context is that the absence of a phone call on Tuesday reflects the ordinary passage of time, rather than an informative component of the event sequence (e.g., a period of conflict between Sally and Jane).

A third assumption is conditional independence. This assumption states that relational events are influenced only by the prior network context and are *not* influenced by possible outcomes. This assumption is most often violated when forward-looking behavior is highly influential. In the case of the Cold War, for instance, nations avoided excessive reactivity because nuclear holocaust was a possible outcome. Assuming that actors were only evaluating prior network contexts *and not* possible outcomes would therefore provide a misleading representation of event activity.

A final assumption is *between* network state dependence. REM, like SAOM, measures endogenous network effects as the network state at the time of network change. Although REM can allow for multiple ties to form in a single moment, it cannot account for within-panel dependencies that might cause multiple ties to form as part of an emergent substructure. Hence, the model may not be appropriate if researchers are interested in within-time dependence.

Model Specification

Table 4.1 presents a number of common statistics that can be incorporated into REM. Statistics can be computed either on the previous network states or on the hypothetical changes to the network. For instance, the inertia statistic is the number of all prior relational events involving a focal dyad, while the transitive triplet statistic measures the number of transitive triplets connected to i that would exist if an ij relational event were to occur. This means that we can include measures that represent the influence of existing network structures or that drive actors to pursue particular changes to the network state. In this respect, we can conceptualize REM as providing an agent-based

Term		Formula	Lower-Order Terms
Node matching	●⟶●	$a_i a_j$	Sender (a), receiver (a)
Node mixing	●⟶○	$a_i b_j$	Sender (a), receiver (b)
Inertia	●⇄●	$\sum_j^{T<t} y_{ij} + \sum_{ji}^{T<t} y_{ji}$	
Reciprocation	○⟷○	$\sum_j^{T=t} y_{ij} y_{ji}$	
Reciprocal node matching	●⟷●	$\sum_j^{T=t} y_{ij} y_{ji} a_i a_j$	Sender (a), receiver (a), reciprocity, node matching
Reciprocal node mixing	●⟷○	$\sum_j^{T=t} y_{ij} y_{ji} a_i b_j$	Sender (a,b), receiver (a,b), reciprocity, incoming node mixing, outgoing node mixing
Two-path		$\sum_j^{T=t} y_{ij} y_{jk}$	
Out-two-star		$\sum_j^{T=t} y_{ij} y_{ik}$	
In-two-star		$\sum_j^{T=t} y_{ij} y_{kj}$	
Three-cycle		$\sum_{j,k}^{T=t} y_{ij} y_{jk} y_{ki}$	Two-path
Transitive triplet		$\sum_{j,k}^{T=t} y_{ij} y_{ik} y_{kj}$	Two-path, in-two-star, out-two-star

Table 4.1   Common REM terms. y is a relational event, and a and b are nodal attributes. Superscript $T = t$ denotes that statistics are computed on hypothetical changes to current network state. Superscript $T < t$ denotes that statistics are computed on the prior network states.

interpretation in specific circumstances (Butts, 2017). The model is also able to include either local or global network statistics.

One characterizing aspect of REM is that it is usually necessary to consider the recency of previous events. Imagine an event sequence spanning decades, such as conflict between nations. It would be unreasonable to expect that the wars that happened generations in the past carry the same weight as war within the past month or year. Lerner, Bussmann, Snijders, and Brandes (2013) propose a weighting function that can be tuned to assign varying influence to more or less recent relational events. Temporal weights are especially useful in event sequences with long observation periods, where older events often have less influence than more recent events. Butts (2008) also proposes a set of *p-shift* parameters that allow for "turn taking" among actors, where actors are only influenced by specific sequences involving other actors. The *p*-shift parameters are especially useful in communication networks (i.e., email chains), where actors often await a response from a specific actor before initiating an additional communication.

Example 4.1. Illegal Drug Trade on the Dark Web

Several years ago, my collaborator Dana Haynie and I scraped illicit drug trade data from an online market on the "dark web"—an encrypted region of cyberspace where illegal drug markets operate using a format similar to eBay (Duxbury & Haynie, 2021a, 2021b). We collected relational event data on drug exchanges connecting dyadic pairs of buyers and vendors operating on the Silk Road 3.1 illegal drug website. Drug exchange data are relational event data in that the ties (drug exchanges) exist in only fleeting moments of continuous time, but the patterning of prior exchanges is likely to influence future trade. Here, we will analyze a subset of the data containing 2,792 marijuana exchanges observed over 14 months of market activity. The network contains 1,712 actors in total: 1,624 buyers and 88 vendors.

Actors on Silk Road 3.1 occupy distinct roles: buyers and vendors. Thus, we can regard the relational event data set as bipartite.[1] We can preprocess our data and implement the models using a combination of the rem and survival packages for R. Another popular R package for relational event analysis is the relevent package. But this package has limited functionality for bipartite event sequences, so we won't use it here. The Chapter 4 supplement provides R code to replicate the example.

Data Preparation

The first step in estimating an REM is constructing the risk set from the event sequence. Prior to preprocessing, our data set looks like a standard edge-list. Since we're working with bipartite data, our "sender" and "receiver"

---

[1]There are no vendor–vendor exchanges in the marijuana exchange data, so the event sequence is not multilevel.

columns contain distinct sets of actors. For a simple subset of three buyers and two vendors, our hypothetical edgelist would look something like this:

$$
\begin{bmatrix}
Buyer & Vendor & Time \\
1 & 3 & 1 \\
1 & 4 & 1 \\
2 & 3 & 1 \\
1 & 3 & 2 \\
2 & 3 & 2 \\
2 & 4 & 2 \\
\vdots & \vdots & \vdots \\
i & j & T
\end{bmatrix}.
$$

Now we expand the edgelist into a fully specified risk set that includes not only the event sequence but also the set of all dyads that *could* be involved in an event. The rem package provides the createRemDataset function to preprocess the data. From here, our hypothetical edgelist expands to

$$
\begin{bmatrix}
Buyer & Vendor & Time & Event \\
1 & 3 & 1 & 1 \\
1 & 4 & 1 & 1 \\
2 & 3 & 1 & 1 \\
2 & 4 & 1 & 0 \\
1 & 3 & 2 & 1 \\
1 & 4 & 2 & 0 \\
2 & 3 & 2 & 1 \\
2 & 4 & 2 & 1 \\
\vdots & \vdots & \vdots & \vdots \\
i & j & T &
\end{bmatrix}.
$$

This reconfiguration includes a fourth column indicating whether an event occurred or not (whether a buyer and vendor were engaged in a drug trade at a particular observation period). The data contain all buyers and vendors who are observed on the market at a given time period and records whether a marijuana exchange occurred between a focal buyer–vendor pair at each observation. The event indicator variable, which indicates here whether a marijuana exchange occurred, acts as the dependent variable for our analysis. Once we've wrangled our data into the correct format, it's a simple matter of merging in time-invariant and time-varying exogenous covariates of interest.

We will include several bipartite network statistics. First, we measure repeated exchange using the inertia statistic first proposed by Butts (2008).

The statistic increases in value when a focal buyer has purchased marijuana from a focal vendor an increasing number of times in the past. Second, we measure four-cycle closure. Four-cycles arise when two buyers share a purchasing history, acting as an indirect referral (Duxbury & Haynie, 2021a, 2021b). The statistic increases in tandem with the number of four-cycles that a hypothetical drug exchange would close if that drug exchange were to occur (Brandenberger, 2018). We will also control for buyers' and vendors' degree centrality.[2] This measure accounts for the total number of drug exchanges a buyer or vendor has previously engaged in.

In addition to network statistics, REM can include time-varying and time-invariant actor characteristics. Two important variables are price and reputation. We construct a time-invariant vendor variable equal to the average price paid in a marijuana exchange, where higher prices mean more costly marijuana purchases on average. Reputations are also important as online drug markets are high-risk environments, and so buyers often flock to trustworthy distributors. We construct the vendor reputation score as a time-varying summary of all sales ratings a vendor has received as of a given month (each ranked on a scale of –5 to 5). Since our timing data are not exact (monthly records), we'll use a discrete time model. Hence, we estimate the REM as a logistic regression.

Analysis

Column 1 of Table 4.2 presents results. The inertia and four-cycles parameters are positive. We can interpret these coefficients in three ways. First, we could conclude that increases in four-cycle closure and inertia (repeated trade) increase the frequency (the hazard ratio) of drug transactions in a given time period. Second, we could conclude that increases in four-cycle closure and inertia increase the *odds* that a transaction will occur between a specific vendor and a specific receiver at a given time period. Third, we could conclude that increases in four-cycle closure and inertia *decrease the timing* to the next drug transaction. Due to the flexible representation of REM as a hazard model, each of these interpretations is supported.

To illustrate each of these interpretations, we begin by focusing on inertia. A one-unit increase in the inertia measure increases the hazard rate of drug trade by 12% ($exp(.113) = 1.12$). This means that the total number of drug exchanges in a time period is expected to increase when histories of repeated

---

[2]We set temporal weights for each network statistic to .7. For guidance on choosing a weight, see either Brandenberger (2018) or Lerner et al. (2013).

	1. Discrete Time REM
Reputation	.003*** (.000)
Price	−.000*** (.000)
Four cycles	.191** (.064)
Inertia	.113* (.044)
Vendor degree	.005*** (.001)
Buyer degree	.267*** (.028)
Akaike information criteria	106,343
Bayesian information criteria	106,382
χ^2	818***

Table 4.2 Discrete time REM of marijuana trade on Silk Road 3.1. Coefficients and standard errors reported.

$*p < .05. **p < .01. ***p < .001.$

exchange are prevalent on the market. In this respect, the interpretation provides us with insight to the *total* prevalence of marijuana trade. To obtain a unit-level interpretation, we could equivalently state that the *odds* that a drug exchange will occur increases by 12% when it connects a buyer–vendor pair that have exchanged drugs more frequently in the past. This interpretation provides us with some insight to which dyads are most likely to engage in marijuana trade at any given time period. Finally, we could also conclude that the timing *between* successive drug exchanges decreases when the next exchange in the event sequence implicates a buyer and vendor who have a history of drug exchange.

Turning to four-cycle closure, a one-unit increase in the four-cycles measure increases the hazard rate by 21% ($exp(.191) = 1.21$). This result tells us that buyers prefer to purchase from vendors who are embedded in similar network clusters, consistent with the indirect referral mechanism. It further suggests that the volume of marijuana trade increases when four-cycle closure becomes more prevalent.

The positive coefficient for buyers' degree centrality indicates that buyers who have purchased frequently in the past have a higher probability of purchasing again at a given observation (shorter timing to next purchase). The positive coefficient for vendors' degree indicates that vendors who have made a large number of drug sales in the past are more likely to be selected for drug purchasing at a given observation, which likely reflects status processes (Podolny, 2010).

Turning to exogenous covariates, the price variable is negative and significant, reflecting a preference for more affordable goods. Consistent with prior studies, the reputation parameter is positive, indicating that buyers tend to prefer high reputation vendors when purchasing marijuana. Each unit increase in vendors' cumulative sales ratings increases the odds of a marijuana exchange involving that vendor by .3% ($exp(.003) = 1.003$).

Model Checking

The fact that REM reduces to logistic regression during estimation means that model-checking practices are quite familiar. Improvements in model fit can be gleaned from comparisons of Akaike and Bayesian information criteria. Brandenberger (2019) provides a simulation method for evaluating overall model fitness. Similar to the model fit assessments described in earlier chapters, the method includes simulating possible event sequences from the data and then evaluating whether the interquartile range of the simulated event sequences contains the observed event sequence.[3]

It bears emphasizing that the identifying assumptions that undergird logistic regression also influence discrete time REM. Such assumptions include no low cell counts, that the likelihood principle is reasonable, and that the logistic functional form of the model is appropriate for the data. Similarly, continuous-time REM is influenced by Cox model assumptions. This includes that the partial likelihood is equal to the maximum likelihood and that no two relational events occur exactly simultaneously. In cases where some events are measured in the same time frame, we can use approximate likelihood estimation strategies, such as Efron's (1974) method. Alternatively, we can allow for simultaneous events using a discrete time model if a large number of events occur in the same time period, such as in the darknet data.

Advanced Interpretation

Like other statistical network models, REM coefficients absorb the variance of omitted variables, even when those variables do not correlate with REM coefficients (Duxbury, 2021c). Consequently, we can't interpret coefficients as effect sizes, compare coefficients between models, or rely on interaction coefficients to evaluate interactions. However, due to REM's close relationship to logistic regression, we are able to utilize a wide variety of tools

---

[3]Current implementations, however, are limited by run times. Simulation of artificial event sequences can take over 3 hours for even moderately sized networks. The method has also yet to be translated into open-source software, and thus results are not reported here.

	1. AME (SE)[a]
Reputation	.001*** (.000)
Price	−.000*** (.000)
Four-cycles	.047** (.016)
Inertia	.028* (.011)
Vendor degree	.001*** (.000)
Buyer degree	.065*** (.07)

Table 4.3   Average marginal effects of marijuana trade on Silk Road 3.1

Note: Delta method standard errors reported. AME = average marginal effect; SE = standard error.
[a] AMEs correspond to the model in column 1 of Table 4.2.
*$p < .05$. **$p < .01$. ***$p < .001$.

to address these issues that aren't always available for statistical network models. These methods include marginal effects (Duxbury, 2021c; Long & Mustillo, 2021; Mize, Doan, & Long, 2019), the likelihood ratio approach of Allison (1999), and the standardization approach of Karlson et al. (2012). Here we'll focus on the average marginal effect.

Table 4.3 (column 1) presents the AME for each REM parameter. The reputation AME is .001, indicating that each 1-point increase in a vendor's reputation score correlates with a .001 increase in the probability that the focal vendor will be involved in a marijuana sale at a given time period. Operating over a range of −15 to 259, this parameter explains substantial variation in the frequency of marijuana purchasing. Similarly, turning to endogenous network effects, we find that each unit increase in the four-cycles measure increases the probability of a marijuana trade by .05, or 5 percentage points. Likewise, each unit increase in the inertia measure increases the probability that a focal buyer and focal vendor will be involved in a marijuana exchange by 3 percentage points.

Missing Data

Missing data pose two types of problems in REM: missing actor attributes and missing tie data. As in TERGM and SAOM, the cardinal sin is listwise deletion. When actors are missing, we get systematic errors in our network statistics that can bias REM coefficients. We can use standard multiple imputation strategies for missing data on node-level attributes. We can also use univariate imputations (mode, median, or mean). Recall that univariate imputations only suppress statistical power, so the procedure does little other than produce conservative coefficients.

Missing tie data in REM are less widely studied. Lerner and Lomi (2020b) study missing dyads in large event sequences, finding that even small samples of large event sequences can reliably estimate REM parameters as long as suitably defined risk sets are sampled. Hence, if the event sequence can be reasonably assumed to contain suitable risk sets and the data set is large, then missing data are a less severe problem.

Other instances of missing tie data may be more complicated. In principle, we can impute missing data using the strategies outlined in earlier chapters. For instance, data missing from left truncation may be imputed using ERGM-based imputation or Bayesian data augmentation (Hipp et al., 2015; Koskinen et al., 2013). Simulation assessments of this type of missingness suggest that ERGM imputation performs better than leaving left truncated data unimputed, but estimates are usually still biased (Duxbury, n.d.). Similarly, the strategy developed by Krause, Huisman, and Snijders (2018) for SAOM could, in principle, be translated to REM (see Chapter 3 for details). This would involve sequentially imputing data for each missing panel by first estimating an REM for the first two time periods, using the coefficients to predict the missing data for the third time period, and repeating this process for the entire event sequence. The results from models fit to the imputed event sequences would then be pooled for final interpretation using Rubin's (1976) rules.

Until further insights are developed, researchers may find it useful to consult multiple strategies. If results are robust using various missing data imputation methods, then researchers can be confident in their robustness. In instances where results from multiple methods do not align, multiply imputed results should generally be preferred over naive estimation of REM with missing tie data, as listwise deletion is generally more problematic than improper imputations.

Other Modeling Considerations

Unobserved Heterogeneity

Readers versed in survival analysis have probably wondered about unobserved heterogeneity—unmeasured node or time period confounders that may affect REM estimates. In REM, we must consider heterogeneity among both senders and receivers. For example, some buyers may purchase marijuana more frequently than others because of an unmeasured characteristic.

Alternatively, some vendors may be more "attractive" for marijuana purchasing than others for an unobserved reason.

The most common strategy for handling these sources of unobserved heterogeneity is to utilize some combination of clustering, frailty, and stratification (Brandenberger, 2018; Butts & Marcum, 2017; Kitts et al., 2017). Each of these strategies represents increasingly aggressive approaches for handling unobserved heterogeneity. Clustering standard errors, for example, corrects standard errors for nesting of events within actors but does little to correct coefficients. Including a frailty term will adjust coefficients and standard errors, but coefficients are biased if the frailty term correlates with any independent variables. Stratification—including a vector of dummy variables for actors—is the most aggressive control and will eliminate all possible sources of confounding on the stratified dimension. However, it also means that researchers cannot analyze any variables on the level of analysis that is stratified. For example, if we include a vector of vendor-level dummy variables in the marijuana exchange data, we would be unable to model *any* time-invariant vendor-level variable.

We can illustrate the utilities and trade-offs of several of these approaches using the Silk Road 3.1 data. To start, we can calculate buyer-clustered standard errors to adjust variance estimates for differences in buyers' activity rates. This correction has no impact on coefficients but will adjust standard errors for differences in buyers' purchasing habits. Column 1 of Table 4.4 presents results from REM with standard errors clustered on buyers. The parameters are unchanged, but now the variance estimates increase. While this doesn't affect substantive conclusions for most coefficients, it is notable that the inertia parameter changes from significant to insignificant once we account for buyer heterogeneity. This may indicate that the positive effect of inertia is confounded with unobserved heterogeneity among buyers.

We may also be concerned with unobserved characteristics of receivers. While the marijuana trade data contain a slew of vendor characteristics, it is possible that some unmeasured vendor characteristic is influencing marijuana trade. We can address this by including a series of vendor dummy variables into our model. This serves the same function as a conventional "fixed-effects" model, where time-invariant vendor-level variables are controlled. Column 2 presents these results. Our primary findings are robust to this specification, but of note is the sharp decrease in Akaike information criteria (AIC) and Bayesian information criteria (BIC). These dramatic improvements in model fit indicate that, even though our primary specifications are robust to vendor fixed effects, the fixed-effects specification improves explanatory power.

	1. Buyer Clustered SE[a]	2. Vendor FE[b]	3. Time Controls[c]
Reputation	.003*** (.000)	.005*** (.000)	.004*** (.000)
Price	−.000*** (.000)	NA	NA
Four-cycles	.191** (.071)	.300*** (.073)	.151 (.085)
Inertia	.113 (.074)	.113 (.066)	.063 (.061)
Vendor degree	.005*** (.001)	.021*** (.002)	−.002 (.002)
Buyer degree	.267*** (.036)	.192*** (.043)	.194*** (.054)
Akaike information criteria	106,343	65,163	65,163
Bayesian information criteria	106,382	65,206	65,215
χ^2	818***	1,349***	2,366***

Table 4.4 Discrete time REM of marijuana trade on Silk Road 3.1 accounting for unobserved heterogeneity. Coefficients and standard errors reported.

Note: SE = standard error; FE = fixed effects; NA = not applicable (variable held constant in model).
[a] Standard errors clustered on sender.
[b] Standard errors clustered on sender, stratified by vendors.
[c] Standard errors clustered on sender, stratified by vendors, linear, quadratic, and cubic time variables included.
**$p < .01$. ***$p < .001$.

Also of note is the four-cycles coefficient in column 2, which increases by about 50% between models. Because changes in coefficients cannot be directly interpreted in REM, we'll use the AME to compare partial effects between models (Table 4.5). The four-cycle closure AME increases from .047 in the original model to .070 in the model that includes vendor fixed effects, an increase of 33%, indicating that unobserved vendor-level heterogeneity suppressed the effect of four-cycles. Interestingly, the AME for vendors' degree triples in size after including vendor fixed effects, suggesting that unobserved vendor heterogeneity suppressed the influence of vendors' degree on buyers' purchasing as well.

Time Trends

Another consideration is spurious trending. If there is a universal trend toward greater event activity and that trend correlates with coefficients of interest, then omitting controls for time trends will bias our estimates. For example,

	1. AME (*SE*)	Percent Change After Including Vendor FE[a]
Reputation	.001*** (.000)	42%
Price	NA	NA
Four-cycles	.070*** (.017)	33%
Inertia	.027 (.016)	−4%
Vendor degree	.005*** (.000)	298%
Buyer degree	.045*** (.010)	−31%

Table 4.5   Average marginal effects of marijuana trade on Silk Road 3.1 for model including vendor fixed effects

Note: AME = average marginal effect; *SE* = standard error; FE = fixed effects; NA = not applicable (variable held constant in model). Delta method standard errors reported.
[a] As compared to AMEs based on model without vendor fixed effects (column 1 of Table 4.3).
***$p < .001$.

in our darknet market, network structure may grow increasingly complex as time passes. Because network structure accrues from histories of exchange, it is possible that an unmeasured time trend correlates with both the volume of marijuana exchanges and the four-cycle and inertia variables. We can account for this possibility by controlling for time. Here we'll control for continuous time by including linear, quadratic, and cubic time specifications. We could also control for time trends by including dummy variables for each time period. The parameters for reputation and buyers' degree are robust after controlling for time, but the four-cycles coefficient and vendors' degree coefficient are rendered insignificant (column 3, Table 4.4). Also of note is that model fit worsens (AIC and BIC increase). This suggests that the model in column 3 may be overfit. Given the decreases in model fit, we would likely prefer the model that does not control for time.

Left Truncation

A final consideration is left truncation. Left truncation occurs when early relational events go unobserved. For example, if we had started our observation period 5 months after Silk Road 3.1 had launched, we would be missing information on the first 5 months of drug exchange. In standard event history analysis, this would only present an issue if the unobserved events substantially differ from the observed events on a host of independent variables. However, in REM, these events are relevant for re-creating the network structure at each time period, and hence their omission introduces nonrandom measurement error into network parameter estimates. The market exchanges that are unobserved create nonrandom patterns of missingness in our endogenous network statistics.

Simulation results suggest that the left truncation bias in endogenous network parameter estimates is often far greater than in standard event history analysis (Duxbury, n.d.). The good news, however, is that the bias can be reduced substantially with dyad fixed effects. The reason is that unobserved dyad-level differences in the network state are time invariant in the sense that they occur prior to observation. We therefore can hold constant the differences between observed and unobserved tie changes by including fixed effects for each dyad. In fact, simulation results suggest that if we stratify our models by dyads and assign large temporal weights to network statistics, we can almost eliminate the bias in network parameter estimates.

An alternative strategy for dealing with left truncation is to specify a rolling time window for the risk set, as proposed by Stadtfeld and Block (2017). The benefit of this strategy is that left truncation cannot bias a properly specified model because, under the assumption of no interactions with time, we only include observations where we have complete information on the relevant network state. This approach works well when we can safely subset our data into precise time windows or when we have prior knowledge of what time windows are reasonable. However, sensitivity to the duration of time windows has not yet been assessed, and it is often not clear what time windows should be specified or what implications misspecified time windows have for results. In the case of darknet drug trade, for instance, it would be reasonable to assume some amount of recency bias. But if a buyer left the market for a year and returned, it would also be reasonable to expect that the buyer would return to the same vendor that they had previously purchased from in the past. If researchers are unsure of what time windows are realistic for the data set or expect time windows of varying length for different actors, dyad stratification may be preferable. Both strategies can also be combined to hold dyad-level differences constant and to only account for the influence of recent events.

Model Extensions

One desirable property of REM is its straightforward extension to bipartite event data, as we saw in the example of darknet drug trade. Brandenberger (2018) also introduces a bipartite REM for nonrepeatable event sequences. In her analysis of policy cosigning among American congressionals, for instance, it is impossible for events to repeat because each bill only comes before Congress once. Her model provides an interpretation similar to classical event history, where parameters can be interpreted as increasing or decreasing the time to first occurrence.

Above we discussed corrections for unobserved heterogeneity in terms of differences in the event rates. But there may also be heterogeneity in the *riskset*. One possible manifestation is that, in large event sequences, actors are only at risk of an event if they occupy a similar position in the network structure. We may have a network of business meetings in multiple organizations in the apparel industry. Most employees are not at risk of coattending business meetings in other organizations. We would therefore have to constrain the risk set so that only specific actors, such as managers or salespeople, can attend interorganizational meetings, while most actors are only at risk of intraorganizational meetings. If we know constraints beforehand, this is straightforward to accomplish by including a vector of indicator variables equal to 1 if two actors are unable to participate in events with one another and equal to 0 otherwise.

If we do not know the sources of unobserved heterogeneity, then it is possible to detect latent clusters of event activity. DuBois, Butts, and Smyth (2013) propose such a framework that integrates stochastic blockmodeling with REM. Their results suggest that incorporating latent clusters increases model fitness in an online direct messaging network. Such corrections are especially useful in large networks where it is unreasonable to expect that all actors are able to connect with one another.

Another appealing property of REM is that the model has direct application to *nondyadic* relational event data. We tend to think of relational events as interactions between pairs of actors, but it is possible to scale REM to polyadic relationships (Butts, 2008; Perry & Wolfe, 2013). Consider wedding planning. A set of actors to be betrothed designates an event and seeks to initiate the event with an audience. In a large wedding, the audience may be many hundreds of people. In a small wedding, perhaps the audience is only several people. However, in only rare cases is the event dyadic. To formulate a polyadic REM, we simply partition the actors into sets of sending groups and receiving groups. In the case of the wedding, we may have the engaged couple as the sender and each individual recipient (or family of recipients) as receivers. Then it is merely a matter of computing relevant network statistics on the grouped data.

Although it is straightforward to formulate a nondyadic REM, software implementations for this case are relatively less developed. The relevent package in R provides utilities for implementing such cases, but network statistics are not well defined, so the functionality is relatively limited. The informR package provides additional utilities for calculating network statistics on complex event sequences.

An Alternative: The Dynamic Network Actor Model

Like network panel models, we can formulate a model for relational event data that espouses an *actor*-based framework. The primary benefit of this framework is that we are able to distinguish between the factors that lead actors to *initiate* events and the factors that lead actors to *choose* specific alters once those events are initiated. Consider the case of direct messaging in online dating platforms. Specific senders may be feeling particularly lonely or lustful, driving them to "swipe right"—elect a possible dating profile as eligible for direct messaging—at a greater rate than other actors. In these cases, we may be especially interested in formulating a model that directly accounts for differences in the rates of senders' outgoing tie activity and receivers' "attractiveness" when senders decide to initiate an event.

Stadtfeld et al. (2017a) first proposed the dynamic network actor model (DyNAM) to examine undirected ties in time-stamped data and have extended the model to directed event data in later work (Stadtfeld & Block, 2017). The key insight in DyNAM is that heterogeneity in sender activity rates may influence who creates ties. Whereas REM regards all active dyads as being at risk of an event during a given observation, DyNAM regards activity rates as unfolding in two distinct phases. First, actors choose whether to initiate an event. Second, after choosing to initiate an event, actors search for suitable alters with whom to coordinate connections. These two processes are visualized and contrasted with REM in Figure 4.2.

Mathematically, DyNAM models the waiting time between two events. We assume an inhomogeneous Poisson process for the waiting period, given by $\psi_{ij}(y|\theta,\beta)$. We then formulate the waiting time as a function of two independent probabilities—the probability that an actor will initiate a relational event and the probability that an alter will be selected given that an event has been initiated:

$$\psi_{ij}(y|\theta,\beta) = \tau_i(y,\theta) \cdot p(ij;y,\beta). \tag{4.3}$$

In this respect, $\psi_{ij}(y|\theta,\beta)$ simply represents the probability that i will initiate a relational event *and* that, once that event has been initiated, will select j as an alter. The probability of an ij relational event occurring is therefore the *joint* probability that a focal actor will search for a tie and will choose a focal alter among a set of available choices.

In practice, we are typically interested in hypothesis testing through parameter inference. We estimate two distinct models, one for the rate function and one for the choice function. The model for the rate function $\tau_i(y,\theta)$ provides the probability that an actor will initiate a relational event:

88

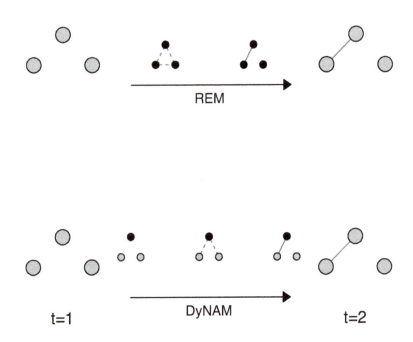

Figure 4.2 Sequencing of event activity in DyNAM and REM. Black nodes indicate that a node is "at risk" of a relational event. Dashed lines reflect what events are possible.

$$\tau_i(y; \theta) = exp(\theta_0 + \sum_k \theta_k r_k(i,y)). \qquad (4.4)$$

From left to right, we can read this equation as providing the probability that i will initiate a relational event as an exponential function of the baseline hazard rate θ_0 and the set of network and actor characteristics that influence actors' activity rates. $r_k(.)$ is a mapping function that calculates k statistics on the exogenous attributes of i and the network y at a given moment in time. θ_k provides the parameter weights for $r_k(i,y)$ that increase or decrease actors' sending rates. For example, in our example of online dating profiles, by interpreting the results for θ_k, we would learn what factors increase or decrease the probability that a specific actor will spend more time searching for eligible dating profiles on the online platform.

The second model is a model for the probability that an actor will select a specific alter once they have begun searching for an alter. In the example of online dating, the model for the choice function tells us which dating profile is most likely to select for direct messaging.

$$f(i,j,y) = \sum_b \beta_b s_b(i,j,y). \tag{4.5}$$

Here, $s_b(.)$ is a mapping function that calculates statistics on the network, the sending actor, and the receiving actor. β_b is a vector containing the parameter weights that increase or decrease the probability that i will initiate an event with j in accordance to a unit increase in the statistics provided in $s_b(i,j,y)$. β_k tells us what factors increase or decrease the probability that an actor will choose to initiate a direct message with another online dater (out of all possible online daters that the actor could message at the same time period).

Because each actor chooses one alter out of a set of possible alters, a discrete choice model makes sense:

$$p(ij;y,\beta) = \frac{exp(f(i,j,y))}{\sum exp(f(i,j',y))}. \tag{4.6}$$

Here, the denominator represents the functions for all alters that were *not* selected. If this model looks familiar, it is because the mathematical formulation of regarding the probability of an event as the product of the rate of senders' activity and multinomial choice is directly informed by SAOM (Stadtfeld et al., 2017a). In practice, the models are estimated using maximum likelihood estimation (Stadtfeld & Block, 2017).

DyNAM may be useful when we are interested in using an actor-oriented interpretation that allows for competing rate functions among actors with heterogeneous motivations. Although an actor-oriented interpretation is available in REM (Butts, 2017), REM does not specifically distinguish the heterogeneity in actors' rate functions from their choice behavior (Stadtfeld & Block, 2017). DyNAM is distinct in that it decomposes the tie initiation and choice phases into two separate coefficients, offering more precise interpretations for each process. If distinct interpretations for the rate function and choice behavior are desirable, DyNAM may be appropriate. DyNAM can be implemented using the goldfish package in R.

Note that DyNAM assumes that alters' characteristics do not influence senders' rate functions. In some instances, this may not be a reasonable assumption. In the context of darknet drug trafficking, drug buyers likely are influenced by their own personal characteristics, such as histories of addiction, Internet savviness, and willingness to pay a higher cost for shipping.

But buyers' activity rates may also be influenced by vendor characteristics. Imagine a market where there are no vendors that distribute heroin. A heroin user would probably not buy from that market or perhaps even start an account. In this scenario and similar ones where alter characteristics determine whether actors are willing to begin searching for alters, the DyNAM will be inappropriate, as it assumes that the rate function and choice function are independent.

When to Use REM?

Models for relational event data are distinct from network panel models in that the data structure, rather than assumptions about generative processes, is a primary determinant of model adequacy. Relational event data contain fine-grained information on timing, and models for relational event data assume that events do not persist across multiple observations unless they are reactivated. Network panel data, by contrast, provide coarse information on timing, and network panel models assume that ties persist across time unless they are changed. Hence, a simple litmus test for whether REM is appropriate is as follows: Do the data measure long-lasting ties (friendships, business relations, kinships, romantic partnerships) with crude timing information? Or, do the data provide fine-grained timing information and ephemeral ties (golf games, market exchanges, phone calls, romantic encounters)? If the answer is the latter, REM will be the preferred model.

A second question is whether to formulate REM as a discrete time or continuous time model. For the Cox model to be appropriate, we have to have *exact* continuous time measurements with no two events occurring simultaneously, although we can tolerate modest violations of this latter assumption using approximate likelihood methods, such as Efron's method (Efron, 1974). In other cases, such as the darknet marijuana trade network, ties may be recorded with a good amount of granularity but are not properly ordered in that exact sequencing is unavailable or that we do not have continuous measures of event activity. In these cases, the discrete time approach (logistic regression) that allows for simultaneous events and only assumes the proper *sequencing* of events is more appropriate.

In terms of adjudicating between DyNAM and REM, some guidance may be found in a recent exchange between the developers of both models (Butts, 2017; Stadtfeld, Hollway, & Block, 2017b). The key distinction between the models comes down to the actor-oriented interpretation. As Butts (2017) observes, REM can be specified in a straightforward fashion to obtain an actor-level interpretation. If our goal is simply to interpret model parameters as reflective of actors' behaviors, we can use either model. However, if our goal is to incorporate actors' *intentions* into the statistical formulation of the model, then DyNAM provides greater utility. Particularly, if we are interested in why activity rates differ between actors, DyNAM would be more flexible in allowing researchers to model and interpret differences in agents' activity rates. Similarly, if we want to know what makes an alter more "attractive," DyNAM would be more precise, as it does not blend alter effects on the rate function with alter effects on the choice function. The trade-off is that DyNAM regards activity rates as independent from choice behavior—an assumption that is violated when actors' activity rates are influenced by alters' attributes.

Some isolated examples also suggest that REM tends to provide better model fit than DyNAM (Stadtfeld & Block, 2017). In some cases, we may be more concerned with parameter interpretation, and so the added complexity of DyNAM's separate rate and nomination functions may be especially appealing. In other cases, we may be more concerned with forecasting or prediction. The improved fit of REM may be useful in these circumstances.

In general, researchers should prefer REM to network panel models when examining relational event data. If researchers are interested in an actor-oriented interpretation and it is reasonable to assume the independence of the rate and choice functions, then DyNAM may be an appealing modeling strategy. Alternatively, if researchers prefer an agnostic interpretation, want a more flexible modeling strategy, or are interested in out-of-sample prediction, REM should be preferred.

Conclusion

Oftentimes, we are able to gather time-stamped data to identify the exact timing of tie changes. In these cases, aggregating ties into network snapshots sacrifices useful information on the timing of network change. REM provides a method for analyzing relational event data. REM accounts for the pacing of events, allows events to form and dissolve in their natural time frame, and can include endogenous network statistics as independent variables. Readers interested in further reading on REM can consult Butts (2008) for a technical introduction. An accessible tutorial can be found in Butts and Marcum (2017). A conceptual discussion of the differences between relational event data and network panel data can be found in Butts (2009) or Kitts (2014). Applied examples of REM can be found in Kitts et al. (2017), Duxbury and Haynie (2021b), Brandenberger (2018), Stadtfeld and Block (2017), and Lerner and Lomi (2020a).

CHAPTER 5. NETWORK INFLUENCE MODELS

Much of the excitement in network modeling has focused on methods for analyzing network structure. But social scientists are just as frequently, if not more frequently, interested in how networks influence actors' behaviors.[1] Take an example from criminology. Edwin Sutherland famously argued that peer influence is responsible for much deviant behavior (Sutherland, 1939). The dependent variable of interest here is not a network variable; it is a behavior. Our *independent* variable of interest is a network variable: peers' deviant dispositions. Hence, the research focus becomes one of network influence. This chapter introduces two common models for analyzing network influence: the temporal network autocorrelation model (TNAM) and the coevolution SAOM.

TNAM and SAOM differ in several important respects, the most important of which regards the problem of *selection* and *influence*. When modeling network influence, we are often interested in how network connections exert influence on a focal actor. However, the data usually only tell us whether actors have become more or less connected to similar peers over repeated observation. This means that our interest in network influence is generically confounded with network selection (Shalizi & Thomas, 2011). An increase in the association between peer behaviors and ego behaviors may reflect peer effects (influence) *or* it may arise because actors choose to create more friendships with similar peers (selection).

TNAM and SAOM offer distinct utilities for handling this problem. Unlike SAOM, TNAM makes no explicit corrections for network selection. This means that we have to disentangle network selection from influence on theoretical grounds or using an instrumental variable. SAOM, on the other hand, explicitly distinguishes the two processes (Steglich et al., 2010) but, in doing so, makes stronger assumptions about underlying change processes. This means that we have to pay careful attention to the nature of our data and the assumptions of our modeling strategy when picking a network influence model and interpreting model output.

---

[1] Behaviors, in this context, are broadly understood to include things like actions, opinions, and attitudes in addition to traditional behaviors (e.g., exercise, smoking).

What Do Network Influence Data Look Like?

Imagine that we are interested in analyzing the effect of triadic closure on change in adolescent smoking behavior in two-wave panel data. We measure smoking behavior as a binary variable and we record the number of triangles each actor is embedded in at each time period. Our data structure would look something like this:

$$
\begin{bmatrix}
PersonPanel & Person & Panel & Smoker? & Triad \\
11 & 1 & 1 & 0 & 1 \\
12 & 1 & 2 & 1 & 2 \\
21 & 2 & 1 & 1 & 1 \\
22 & 2 & 2 & 1 & 1 \\
31 & 3 & 1 & 0 & 1 \\
32 & 3 & 2 & 0 & 0 \\
\vdots & \vdots & \vdots & \vdots & \vdots \\
it & i & t & --- & ---
\end{bmatrix}
$$

The main goal of our analysis is to figure out whether change in actors' smoking behavior can be explained, in part, by change in network structure. The unit of analysis is the person panel.

The core statistical issue is controlling for nonindependence among the observations. In the above example, each triad statistic contains three actors, meaning that standard errors from a logistic regression of smoking behavior on triads would be downwardly biased. The complexity of this nesting structure grows as network size increases and as a larger number of network statistics are included into the model. This means that the nesting structure is usually too complex and too idiosyncratic to the model specification to rely on a multilevel model, which may be unestimable or not account for the full range of cross-level dependencies. Further, the fact that we sample from a single network means that we do not preserve random sampling principles that inform standard survey panel designs. Actors may be similar to one another on a range of measured and unmeasured characteristics for spurious or systematic reasons.

The key challenge, then, is how to adjust standard errors for interdependence. Historically, nonparametric methods, such as permutation, were the go-to method for null hypothesis testing . Nonparametric methods have generally fallen out of favor due to computational expensiveness, because nonparametric p values do not support population-level inference outside of specific limiting conditions and because nonparametric models usually cannot include network statistics as independent variables. This chapter focuses on parametric models for network influence. These models are typically less computationally expensive than nonparametric strategies, control for nonindependence among observations, support process-oriented statistical inference, and can include network statistics on the right-hand side of the equation.

The Temporal Network Autocorrelation Model (TNAM)

Imagine momentarily that we are not interested in a network but instead another form of interdependence: spatial contiguity between counties. Say we are analyzing the diffusion of some particular policy between county-level municipalities. The problem that we encounter is *spatial autocorrelation*, referring to the tendency for spatially contiguous counties to be similar to one another for unmeasured reasons. If we fit a linear regression without correcting for spatial autocorrelation, our standard errors would be downward biased and our coefficients may be biased if there is an unmeasured variable causing similarities between observed units.

This same issue was first introduced to the world of network analysis by Doreian (1981), where the problem is known as *network autocorrelation*. Network autocorrelation is correlation between the measurements of a given actor and other actors in the network. Network autocorrelation introduces two problems. First, network autocorrelation causes downward biased standard errors, meaning that a regression fit to data sampled from a complete network will usually provide excessively generous assessments of statistical significance. Second, although autocorrelation does not bias coefficients in itself, network autocorrelation often arises because a control is not included into the model that causes similarities between sampled actors. In this case, even though autocorrelation does not bias coefficients, the absence of an adequate control for the cause of autocorrelation can bias coefficients.

The temporal network autocorrelation model (TNAM) is a relatively simple approach for dealing with these issues in panel data samples from complete networks. The heart of the solution is to control for the network dependencies in an attribute of interest (Doreian, 1981; Hays, Kachi, & Franzes, 2010; Leenders, 2002). Let y be a continuous attribute measured on actor i at time t, and let W be the time-varying adjacency matrix containing the repeated network measures. TNAM can be represented as

$$y = \beta^T z(x, W) + \psi^T W y + e. \tag{5.1}$$

Here $z(x, W)$ is the set of time-varying and time-invariant statistics computed on the repeated network measurements (clustering, degree, functions of alters' attributes) and exogenous attributes (race, gender, class). The β coefficients are identical to a standard linear model. They represent the average change in y given a one-unit increase in $z(x,W)$.

The key distinction between a conventional linear regression and TNAM is the weight matrix, Wy, that controls for network interdependence in y. ψ is an autoregressive (AR) parameter for network autocorrelation. The greater the absolute value of ψ, the greater the amount of interdependence. Large positive AR parameters mean that focal actors' attributes are highly correlated with their peers' attributes, while negative values indicate that actors' attributes are highly dissimilar to their peers. When $\psi = 0$, the TNAM in Equation 5.1 becomes a linear regression.

The model in Equation 5.1 captures an AR(1) process: It only includes network autocorrelation out to a single connection (ego's alters). However, there are instances where we may need to alter or test the adequacy of this specification. Network influence may travel out to path lengths of 2, 3, or longer, giving rise to an AR(2), AR(3), or higher-order autocorrelation process. Further, there may be multiplex network influence, where actors are affected by connections in multiple networks. If the model does not include these higher-order AR processes, estimates will be biased. Strategies for testing and including higher-order AR processes are discussed later in this chapter.

Due to the similarities between TNAM and linear models, it is straightforward to extend the model to discrete outcomes. Let y be a binary response variable. We represent the generalized TNAM as

$$Pr(y = 1) = F(\beta^T z(x,W) + \psi^T Wy). \tag{5.2}$$

Here, we replace y with the probability that an observed it observation is 1 instead of 0. $F(.)$ is the cumulative distribution function. If we assume a logistic function for $F(.)$, we obtain a logistic regression for TNAM. If we assume a probit function, we obtain a probit regression. We use the same process to obtain related generalized linear models, such as Poisson, negative binomial, multinomial, and ordinal regression models. TNAM is typically estimated using maximum likelihood, although Bayesian estimation is also possible (Dittrich, Leenders, & Mulder, 2020).

The Intuition

The simplest way to think of TNAM is as a pooled panel model. The sole difference between TNAM and pooled panel models is that we include the weight matrix on the right-hand side of the equation and can include network statistics that would otherwise have downward biased standard errors. In fact, if we exclude the weight matrix and network statistics from Equations 5.1 and 5.2, the models reduce to a pooled panel model. Hence, without sacrificing complexity, we can think of TNAM as a pooled panel model with a control for network autocorrelation. Coefficients can be interpreted in the same fashion as they would be interpreted using a generalized linear model of the same family (e.g., as increasing the log-odds for logistic regression).

Assumptions

Because TNAM relates closely to a pooled panel model, it inherits many of the same assumptions. Coefficients are only identified under a strict exogeneity restriction, which is violated when there is at least one omitted variable, systematic measurement error, or the model has the incorrect functional form, although the model is tolerant to weak violations of this assumption (Wooldridge, 2002). The model also assumes that there is no unobserved heterogeneity among actors or among time periods. This assumption is usually untenable, although we will discuss strategies for dealing with unobserved unit-level and time heterogeneity in the following sections. TNAM estimates can also be biased due to a misspecified temporal lag structure or when a lagged dependent variable is included without using the appropriate estimator (Nickell, 1981; Vaisey & Miles, 2017).

A multitude of corrections exist for each of these issues, such as including random effects, unit fixed effects, detrending the data, or changing estimators, each of which require their own identifying assumptions. It is not possible to review the full suite of solutions for each issue here, as panel data analysis is an active field in itself. Recent discussions of strategies for dealing with each of these common issues in panel data analysis, the merits of each strategy, and their assumptions can be found in Bollen and Brand (2010), Leszczensky and Wolbring (2019), or Duxbury (2021b).

A unique assumption to TNAM is that we must assume that the network lag structure is properly specified. As in other spatial and temporal autoregressive models, we have to specify a separate autoregressive parameter for each lag length. An AR(1) process means that we only control for alters' similarities but do not control for similarities that may extend beyond ego's immediate connections. We can include higher-order AR processes to account for indirect influences (Dow, 2007). For instance, an AR(3) process would control for similarities between ego and the alters of alters' alters. If we specify only a single network lag, but there is in fact network influence operating out to a path length of 4, our coefficients will most likely be biased (because we do not control for higher-order network autocorrelation), and our standard errors will be downward biased. In practice, we can determine an appropriate lag structure in a stepwise fashion by estimating separate models that sequentially increase the lag structure and by retaining the best-fitting model (Leenders, 2002).

TNAM also assumes no unmeasured network autocorrelation (Dittrich et al., 2020; Dow, 2007). If actors are embedded in two evolving networks that imply different amounts of autocorrelation, but only the weight matrix for one of those networks is controlled, we will get downward biased standard errors and may get biased coefficients from omitted variables. For instance, if a student is friends with smokers and their family member also smokes, we will likely overestimate the network autocorrelation between the student's smoking behavior and their peer smoking behavior if we do not also control for family members' smoking behavior.

Model Specification

TNAM offers a great deal of flexibility in terms of how the model can be specified. The model can include both time-varying and time-invariant exogenous actor attributes as well as network statistics. Moreover, since the dependent variable is not endogenous to the network statistics, we are able to specify both within- and between-panel dependencies by including temporal lags on the time-varying network statistics. Some common network statistics are defined in Table 5.1.

A key distinction between TNAM and other network panel models is that the unit of analysis is the *actor* panel, rather than the *dyad* panel. This means that any network statistics must be calculated as *actor*-level measures. For instance, contrast the triad statistic in Table 5.1 to statistics defined in earlier chapters. Whereas TERGM, SAOM, and REM would measure the hypothetical change in triad counts if a focal tie were to form, the clustering coefficient in Table 5.1 is the proportion of closed triangles in an actor's local neighborhood (Watts & Strogatz, 1998). We therefore have to focus our interpretation on actor-level processes instead of tie-level processes.

An additional utility of TNAM is that we can normalize W to specify theoretically informed network autocorrelation processes (Leenders, 2002; Valente, 1995). Normalization involves dividing W by the row or column sums (outdegree or indegree). Normalization is useful in cases where we are interested in a substantive interpretation for ψ and when we expect alters' influence to either increase or decrease as a function of the number of other actors that alters influence. For instance, row normalization

98

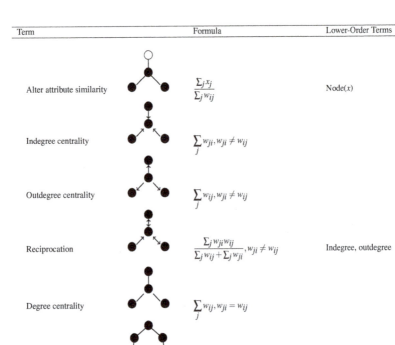

Term	Formula	Lower-Order Terms
Alter attribute similarity	$\dfrac{\sum_j x_j}{\sum_j w_{ij}}$	Node(x)
Indegree centrality	$\sum_j w_{ji}, w_{ji} \neq w_{ij}$	
Outdegree centrality	$\sum_j w_{ij}, w_{ji} \neq w_{ij}$	
Reciprocation	$\dfrac{\sum_j w_{ji} w_{ij}}{\sum_j w_{ij} + \sum_j w_{ji}}, w_{ji} \neq w_{ij}$	Indegree, outdegree
Degree centrality	$\sum_j w_{ij}, w_{ji} = w_{ij}$	
Betweenness centrality	$\dfrac{\sum_{i \neq j \neq k} d_{jk}(i)}{d_{jk}}$	Degree centrality
Clustering coefficient	$\sum_{j,k} w_{ij} w_{ji} w_{jk} \cdot \dfrac{1}{\sum_j w_{ij}(\sum_j w_{ij} - 1)}$	Degree centrality

Table 5.1   Common TNAM terms. w is network tie connecting actors i and j, x is a nodal attribute, and $d_{jk}(i)$ computes the number of shortest path lengths connecting j and k that include i.

implies that ego is influenced by the *average* amount of smoking behavior among alters, while column normalization implies that the influence of alters' smoking behavior is decentralized among each alter's alters (a weak influence process). A detailed discussion of normalization can be found in Leenders (2002).

Example 5.1. A Network Influence Model of Adolescent Smoking Behavior

We'll now formulate a TNAM to examine network influence on adolescent smoking behavior. The data are from the Teenage Friendship and Lifestyle Study. The data contain three waves of measures on network and smoking behavior on 50 female high school students, giving us 150 student panels for analysis. Our dependent variable is a binary indicator of whether a student smokes regularly (more than once per week) in a given panel. For this example, we'll be relying primarily on the tnam package for R. Another popular package for estimating network autocorrelation models is the sna package, but the package is limited to linear models. Since the unique aspect of TNAM is the time-varying weight matrix, we also do not need to rely on either of these specialized software packages to estimate TNAM. We could manually calculate the time-varying weight matrix and any network statistics we want to include using our preferred network software (e.g., UCINET, Pajek, statnet) and then estimate the model with generic regression software (e.g., R, Stata). The primary benefit to estimating the model in R is that the tnam package provides greater utilities for diagnosing higher-order AR processes and calculating relevant network statistics than are available in other software packages. Code to replicate this example is available in the Chapter 5 supplement.

Data Preparation

The first step is to arrange our data into a format that tnam works with. We'll sort the adjacency matrices for each network panel into a sequentially ordered list, such that the first entry is the first panel and the last entry is the last panel. tnam also requires that the dependent variable is provided as a dataframe object with each column representing a single network panel. With our data arranged, we can compute relevant statistics on the network state. The ? "tnam-terms" command allows us to see the terms available. We can also compute relevant statistics using other packages, such as network or igraph, and integrate them into our data set if there is a statistic not available within tnam.

   The most critical metric for our purposes is the time-varying weight matrix, which is the cross-product of the time-varying adjacency matrix and the time-varying smoking behavior variable. We can calculate the weight matrix using the netlag command. To start, we'll specify a simple AR(1) process, although we will test this specification later.

Next, we'll include several exogenous attributes and network statistics of interest. First, we'll include ego's alcohol consumption as an independent variable. The metric is an ordinal measure ranging from 1 to 5, where higher values indicate more frequent alcohol consumption (1 is no alcohol use, 5 is more than one drink per week). We'll also compute several centrality statistics, including indegree centrality, outdegree centrality, and betweenness centrality, to evaluate whether changes in measures of popularity and brokerage influence smoking behavior. Finally, we'll include a measure of triadic closure to evaluate whether changes in group cohesion influence actors' smoking behavior. We measure triadic closure at the ego level using the local clustering coefficient (Watts & Strogatz, 1998). The measure increases in value as the number of triangles in ego's local neighborhood increases.

Analysis

Before estimating models, we'll want to make sure network autocorrelation actually exists. We can test for network autocorrelation using Moran's I. The results from this procedure tell us whether we need to control for network autocorrelation or whether it is weak enough to ignore. Test statistics are significant for each wave of data (Wave I, $p = .01$; Wave II, $p = .006$; Wave III, $p = .006$), reflecting significant levels of network autocorrelation. TNAM is therefore the correct model choice.

Once the measures are prepared, we can estimate the model as a logistic regression. Results are presented in Table 5.2. The negative intercept means that the conditional probability of being a smoker is quite low. When all covariates are held at 0, the probability that a student will be a smoker at a given panel is .026 ($logit^{-1}(-3.64) = .026$). The positive coefficient for alcohol use means that alcohol consumption is positively correlated with smoking. Each increase in the ordinal alcohol consumption scale is associated with a 2.65 ($exp(.975) = 2.65$) times increase in the odds of being a smoker.

We also see negative influence from students' outdegree. This tells us that students who have more outgoing friendships (nominate a greater number of alters as friends) also have a lower likelihood of smoking. The odds of being a smoker at a given panel observation decreases by 61% ($exp(-.953) = .388$) for each additional outgoing friendship tie. Consistent with autocorrelation tests, the AR(1) parameter is positive and significantly different from 0. With a value of .643, we can conclude that there is significant network autocorrelation. This means that there is a strong association between actors' smoking behavior and the smoking behavior of their alters.

1. TNAM of Smoking Behavior	
Alcohol use	.975*** (.236)
Indegree	.026 (.177)
Outdegree	−.953* (.438)
Betweenness centrality	.001 (.004)
Clustering coefficient	−.312 (1.266)
AR(1) parameter	.643* (.252)
Intercept	−3.911*** (.878)
AIC	155.26
BIC	176.34

Table 5.2 TNAM of smoking behavior in three-wave panel data of the Teenage Friendship and Lifestyle Study. Coefficients and standard errors reported.

$*p < .05.$ $***p < .001.$

Missing Data

Missing data is a less severe problem in TNAM as compared to the network models discussed in prior chapters. Since the primary machinery of the model does not rely on complete network data, it is more tolerant to listwise deletion under the assumption of random missingness, with one important caveat. If we are to use listwise deletion, we need to compute network statistics and the weight matrix *prior* to deletion. If we delete observations with missing data prior to calculating network statistics and the weight matrix, then our network measures and measures of network autocorrelation can have nonrandom measurement error, which can bias coefficients for the network statistics of interest. We can also use multiple imputation to impute missing data for actor-level attributes using standard procedures or use the method of Honaker and King (2010) to incorporate network autocorrelation and temporal autocorrelation into the imputations.

Missing tie data are more difficult to handle. Missing tie data influence not only the statistics we calculate on the network structure but also the value of the weight matrix. However, few studies have evaluated the robustness of TNAM estimates of AR parameters or coefficients for network statistics in the presence of missing tie data. Until further wisdom is gained on the subject, researchers may be able to use the model-based imputation methods described in prior chapters if they are concerned with missing tie data. We may, for instance, use ERGM to impute missing tie data at each wave

(Robins et al., 2004). Alternatively, we could use the SAOM imputation procedure described in Chapter 3 to impute missing tie data and pool them with Rubin's (1976) rule (Krause, Huisman, & Snijders, 2018). These suggestions come with the cautionary word that such procedures have not been evaluated for TNAM. While empirical assessments suggest that imputation is preferred to listwise deletion for measuring network structure (Koskinen et al., 2013; Smith & Moody, 2013; Smith et al., 2017), further work is needed to provide firm recommendations in the case of TNAM.

Other Modeling Considerations

Unobserved Heterogeneity

As a pooled panel model, TNAM inherits many of the issues related to unobserved heterogeneity that can influence parameter estimates in conventional panel data analysis. Unobserved unit-level and time heterogeneity, for instance, are common problems. Due to TNAM's close relationship to generalized linear models, it is straightforward to address these issues.

We can start by estimating our TNAM in a multilevel framework to allow for node-level random variation in addition to network autocorrelation. The model in column 1 of Table 5.3 includes a node-level frailty term. The declines in AIC and BIC from the earlier model reveal that model fit has improved, suggesting that there is node-level heterogeneity in our data. Indeed, the variance component for the frailty term is 4.022. Including the frailty term also alters some of our results. Now the AR parameter is not significant, nor is the outdegree coefficient, which implies that the significance of both parameters may have to do with unmeasured variation between actors. The alcohol use coefficient is robust to unobserved node-level variation.

The frailty model assumes that the time-varying covariates are uncorrelated with the unobserved unit-level heterogeneity (Wooldridge, 2002). This assumption is usually violated. We can allow for correlation between the unit-level heterogeneity and independent variables by including $n - 1$ node-level dummy variables into the model. This model is analogous to a fixed-effects model (in the econometric sense) for panel data, where all possible time-invariant differences are held constant but with the addition of the weight matrix and network statistics.

Column 2 of Table 5.3 reports results from models that include node-level fixed effects. We see that results are unchanged in terms of direction and significance, but now we have to change our interpretation to reflect the new model specification. Since we have eliminated time-invariant differences, the coefficients now reflect *within-unit* change. For instance, a one-unit within-

	1. Node RE	2. Node FE[a]	3. Node RE + Time
Alcohol use	1.482*** (.440)	1.703* (.753)	1.488*** (.443)
Indegree	.118 (.177)	.516 (.370)	.105 (.264)
Outdegree	−.778 (.641)	1.266 (1.530)	−.759 (.646)
Betweenness centrality	−.003 (.007)	−.022 (.013)	−.002 (.007)
Clustering coefficient	.415 (1.960)	.567 (5.547)	.505 (1.962)
AR(1) parameter	.574 (.375)	−.721 (.862)	.547 (.381)
Time			.202 (.351)
Intercept	−6.530*** (1.920)	−6.504* (3.079)	−6.935*** (2.085)
Node-level frailty[b]	4.022		4.146
Akaike information criteria	147.06	159.68	148.74
Bayesian information criteria	171.15	328.28	175.84

Table 5.3 TNAM of smoking behavior in three-wave panel data of the Teenage Friendship and Lifestyle Study that correct for unobserved heterogeneity. Coefficients and standard errors reported.

Note: FE = fixed effects; RE = random effects.
[a] Fixed-effect coefficients not reported.
[b] Variance component reported.
$*p < .05$. $***p < .001$.

student increase in the frequency of self-reported alcohol consumption correlates with a 5.5-fold ($exp(1.703) = 5.49$) increase in the odds that a student will change their smoking behavior (transition from a nonsmoker to a smoker or vice versa). Although the fixed-effects specification is more robust to confounders, it also increases the risk of overfitting by including 49 ($n − 1 = 49$) dummy variables. Indeed, the substantial increases in AIC and BIC indicate that the fixed-effects model is performing worse than the random-effects model. Hence, using the criteria of Bollen and Brand (2010), we should prefer the random-effects specification.

A third concern is unobserved time heterogeneity arising from unmeasured differences between the repeated measurements (Duxbury, 2021b). We can account for this by controlling for time trends, either by including time dummy variables or continuous time variables. In column 3 of Table 5.3, we include node random effects alongside a control for the time trend. The linear time trend is nonsignificant, and model fit does not improve. Thus, we can safely exclude the control for time from our model. Our preferred model would be the model in column 1.

Higher-Order Network Autocorrelation

Another consideration is whether there are unmeasured higher-order AR processes. Actors may not only be correlated at a path length of 1 but at higher-order path lengths of 2, 3, 4, and so on, giving rise to AR(2), AR(3), AR(4), and higher-order autoregressive processes. We can test for higher-order network autocorrelation in a stepwise fashion by sequentially including higher-order autocorrelation structures and evaluating improvements in model fit (Leenders, 2002). For an AR(2) process, this would involve creating a second weight matrix, W_2y, where W_2 is an n x n matrix where cells are equal to 1 if two actors are connected at a path length of 2 and are equal to 0 otherwise. We would then include W_2y as an independent variable in our regression *in addition* to Wy. The resulting parameter estimates for each respective variable reflect the strength of AR(1) and AR(2) autocorrelation. We determine which specifications to retain and which to exclude by comparing improvements in model fit as each higher-order autocorrelation structure is included into the model, preferring whichever specification provides the best model fit.

Table 5.4 presents the results from specification tests that include higher-order AR processes in addition to the AR(1) specification. We see modest increases in both AIC and BIC as path lengths increase, reflecting worsening model fit. This suggests that the more parsimonious AR(1) specification adequately captures any relevant network autocorrelation in the data. Consistent with this interpretation, the autocorrelation parameters for both higher-order path distances are nonsignificant. We can therefore conclude that an AR(1) process is appropriate.

	1. Akaike Information Criteria	2. Bayesian Information Criteria
Path distance = 1	155.26	176.34
Path distance = 2	155.62	179.90
Path distance = 3	156.97	184.06

Table 5.4 Model fit comparisons for TNAM with up to three path lengths

Bias in TNAM AR Estimates

A final modeling consideration is network density. TNAM typically underestimates network autocorrelation in dense networks (Dow, Burton, & White, 1982; Mizruchi & Neuman, 2008; Neuman & Mizruchi, 2010). The conservative bias is unlikely to be a problem in most networks of moderate size, as density tends to decline along with network size while the conservative bias in AR parameters is unaffected by network size (Mizruchi & Neuman, 2008; Neuman & Mizruchi, 2010). In our case, the network densities for the three panels are .09 for Wave I, .09 for Wave II, and .10 for Wave III, suggesting that conservative bias in the AR parameters is not severe despite the small size of the network.

Model Extensions

One of the primary appeals of TNAM is its flexibility. The model has straightforward extensions to a number of realistic scenarios. The tnam package, for instance, provides specialized functions for calculating autoregressive parameters from valued edge data. The model can also be applied to bipartite network data by using the affiliation matrix to construct the weight matrix (Fujimoto, Chou, & Valente, 2011). TNAM can also be specified to include multiple network influence mechanisms by including multiple weight matrices for each of the network influence processes of interest (Anselin, 2001; Elhorst, Lacombe, & Piras, 2012).

Coevolution Models: SAOM for Behavioral and Network Change

TNAM is a discrete time model. We therefore implicitly assume that the observed variation in network structure is representative, or at least not systematically misrepresentative, of the unobserved variation in network structure. This assumption may be untenable if there are large time windows between repeated measurements. Perhaps the most substantial limitation of TNAM is that the AR parameter can only tell us whether actors' own behaviors correlate with other actors in the network. Such associations confound dynamic processes of selection and influence, either of which might produce network autocorrelation (Mouw, 2006; Shalizi & Thomas, 2011). Consequently, TNAM is usually unable to distinguish whether network selection or network influence is the cause of network autocorrelation.

Snijders, Steglich, and Schweinberger (2007) extended the stochastic actor-oriented model (SAOM) introduced in Chapter 3 to deal with this type of interdependency. The coevolution model proposed by Snijders et al. (2007)

and popularized by Steglich et al. (2010) uses an actor-oriented framework to model the simultaneous development ("coevolution") of behavior and network change. The model applies to special cases of change in actors' behaviors where actors can be reasonably assumed to have control over the behavior of interest and that change in that behavior is a function of purposeful decision-making. The coevolution approach improves upon alternative frameworks for modeling selection and influence processes by allowing for network dependence among actors, allowing for behavioral and network change to be endogenous, and accounting for unobserved changes in network and behavioral states between network panels.

The coevolution SAOM builds naturally upon the conventional SAOM described in Chapter 3. The heart of the coevolution model is to simultaneously estimate two functions: a network function for network change and a behavioral function for behavior change. Since the network function is almost identical to the SAOM presented in Chapter 3, we'll direct more attention to the behavioral function here. Readers may find it helpful to review Chapter 3 before proceeding, as many details about SAOM assumptions, estimation, and the logic lying underlying SAOM are outlined in more detail in Chapter 3.

Let ρ_i^{net} be the rate function determining whether an actor will be offered a tie change opportunity at a given micro-step and let ρ_i^{beh} be the rate function determining whether an actor will be offered the opportunity to change a *behavior* during a micro-step. We can represent the probability that an actor will be offered the opportunity to change an outgoing tie as

$$\rho_i^{net}/\rho^{total} \tag{5.3}$$

and the probability that an actor will have the opportunity to change a behavior as

$$\rho_i^{beh}/\rho^{total}, \tag{5.4}$$

where $\rho^{total} = \sum_i (\rho_i^{net} + \rho_i^{beh})$. As in standard SAOM, the rate function is typically uniform (e.g., $\rho_i^{beh} = \rho_i^{net} = 1/n$), although this assumption is straightforward to modify.

The rate function tells us whether an actor will have the opportunity to change a behavioral state at a given micro-step, but the objective function determines whether an actor will choose to increase or decrease their behaviors. The behavioral objective function is given by

$$f_i^{beh}(x,y,z) = \sum_k \beta_k^{beh} s_k^{beh}(x,y,z). \tag{5.5}$$

Here, x represents the exogenous attributes provided by the researcher, y is the network state at a given micro-step, and z is the behavioral state at a given micro-step. $s_k^{beh}(x,y,z)$ can be understood to represent the various network and actor characteristics expected to influence changes in actors' behaviors, including exogenous attributes, network statistics, and statistics calculated on the evolving behavioral state. The behavioral objective function in Equation 5.5 can be understood as the values that *would* arise *if* a focal actor were to change their behavior. In this regard, we assume that actors pursue the behavioral states that maximize their preferences. The β coefficients can be interpreted as increasing or decreasing the log-odds that a student will choose to increase/decrease their behavioral state by one unit when $f_i^{beh}(x,y,z)$ increases in value.

We formulate the probability that an actor will choose to increase or decrease a behavior at a given micro-step as a product of the rate function and multinomial probability:

$$\frac{\rho_i^{beh}}{\rho^{total}} \cdot \frac{exp(f_i^{beh}(x,y,z))}{\sum_{z'} exp(f_i^{beh}(x,y,z'))}, \tag{5.6}$$

where $\frac{\rho_i^{beh}}{\rho^{total}}$ gives the probability that an actor will be given the opportunity to increase or decrease their behavior. The numerator of the multinomial probability is the value of the objective function for the possible behavioral change that yields the greatest increase in the objective function for all possible changes to i's behavioral state. The denominator is the sum over the objective behavioral functions for all changes to the behavioral state that *do not* maximize the objective function. Actors can also choose not to change a behavior if there are no behavioral changes that would increase the value of the behavioral objective function.

The coevolution specification provides a slight modification to the network function introduced in Chapter 3. Now the objective function for network change is given by

$$f_i^{net}(x,y,z) = \sum_k \beta_k^{net} s_k^{net}(x,y,z), \tag{5.7}$$

with the probability that an outgoing tie will change at a given micro-step:

$$\frac{\rho_i^{net}}{\rho^{total}} \cdot \frac{exp(f_i^{net}(x,y,z))}{\sum_{y'} exp(f_i^{net}(x,y',z))}, \tag{5.8}$$

where $\frac{\rho_i^{net}}{\rho^{total}}$ is the probability that an actor will have the opportunity to change a network tie and $\frac{exp(f_i^{net}(x,y,z))}{\sum_{y'} exp(f_i^{net}(x,y',z))}$ is the probability that an actor will choose to alter an outgoing tie.

Thus, the two key differences between this probability model and the model presented in Chapter 3 are that we now incorporate competing rate functions for network and behavioral change and we now include statistics computed on the endogenously evolving behavioral state into our equation for network change. Coevolution models can be estimated using method of moments (Snijders et al., 2007), generalized method of moments (Amati et al., 2015), maximum likelihood estimation (Snijders, Koskinen, & Schwein-berger, 2010), or within a Bayesian framework (Koskinen & Snijders, 2007).

The Intuition

We can regard the coevolution SAOM as a multivariate generalized linear model. As in standard SAOM, the coevolution model is formulated in an imputation stage and estimation stage. In the imputation stage, we simulate the unobserved change sequence to the network and behavioral states, allowing actors to change their behaviors and outgoing network ties. This provides us with a simulated data set of micro-steps for estimation. Then, in the estimation stage, we fit a multivariate multinomial logistic regression to the imputed data set. Behavioral function coefficients are interpreted as the log-odds that an actor will choose to increase/decrease the value of the behavioral outcome by one interval.

The inclusion of *both* the evolving network and behavioral states offers some important utilities unavailable in any other model. Imagine that we are interested in evaluating whether friends' smoking behavior causes ado-lescents to change their smoking behavior. We measure friends' smoking behavior as a summary statistic, such as the mean smoking behavior of alters. This statistic would change in value depending on whether (1) a student's friends change their own smoking behavior and (2) a student changes their network composition by withdrawing or forming new ties. By treating both z and y as endogenously evolving, the coevolution model allows both behavioral and network states to independently change as a function of both of these processes, despite that many of these changes are not recorded by panel data.

Coevolution models can account for binary, ordinal, and unordered dis-crete outcome variables (Snijders et al., 2007; Steglich et al., 2010). Coevo-lution models have also been recently extended to allow for continuous outcomes as well (Niezink, Snijders, & van Duijn, 2019), although coefficients in the continuous case have to be interpreted as moving actors' trajectories—that is, the equilibrium state of actors' behavior—instead of as increasing/decreasing the log-odds of behavioral change. For a detailed discussion of interpretation when continuous behaviors are included, see Niezink et al. (2019).

Assumptions

The coevolution formulation of SAOM makes all of the same assumptions as the SAOM described in Chapter 3, including but not limited to agent-driven network change, sequential ordering of tie changes, and continuous time. The coevolution model extends many of these assumptions to the behavioral change process. In particular, coevolution models assume that behavioral change is a *discrete* occurrence in *continuous* time. This means that gradual changes, such as shifts in political attitudes over the course of college, may be ill-suited to the coevolution formulation.

A second key assumption is that behavioral change is sequentially ordered. This means that no two behavioral changes occur in the exact same moment in time. In our example of smoking behavior, this assumption would be violated if two students transition from being "nonsmokers" to smokers simultaneously.[2] In practice, weak violations of this assumption can be tolerated, but if simultaneous behavioral changes are common, then SAOM is inappropriate. For example, the SAOM behavioral function should not be used to study co-offending, since co-offending is collective behavior. SAOM also does not allow for simultaneous changes of network *and* behavioral states.

A third key assumption is that behavioral changes are a function of actors' boundedly rational choice behavior, where actors pursue the behavioral states that maximize their preferences (as defined by the researcher). Consequently, behavioral changes that are *not* the outcome of choice behavior will be ill-suited to the model. For instance, it might be reasonable to formulate a coevolution model predicting the change from unemployment to employment status, where actors seek out employment as a function of network change. But it would be less reasonable to formulate a coevolution model predicting whether an employee gets fired. The decision to fire employees is

---

[2]When I was in high school, my friends and I would pool our money to buy and share cigarettes. Our smoking behavior was necessarily joint behavior because none of us could afford to smoke on our own and because we only smoked when around each other.

outside of the control of employees or only the indirect product of behaviors that employees can control (productivity, workflow).

Model Specification

Coevolution models offer a range of statistics than can be computed on the endogenously evolving network and behavioral states. The range of selection effects described in Chapter 3 can be calculated on the behavioral dependent variable and included in the network function. In addition, coevolution models also allow for a range of statistics that can be computed on the network state and included into the behavioral function to examine network influence on behavioral change. Some of the more popular statistics are presented in Table 5.5.

Term	Formula	Lower-Order Terms
Total alter behavior	$\sum_j y_{ij} z_j$	
Average alter behavior	$\frac{\sum_j y_{ij} z_j}{\sum_j y_{ij}}$	
Total alter similarity	$\sum_j (1 - |z_i - z_j|)$	
Average alter similarity	$\frac{\sum_j (1 - |z_i - z_j|)}{max(z) - min(z)}$	
Isolate	$z_i (1 - max_j(y_{ij}))$	
Indegree	$z_i \sum_j y_{ji}$	
Outdegree	$z_i \sum_j y_{ij}$	
Reciprocal degree	$z_i \sum_j y_{ij} y_{ji}$	Indegree, outdegree, alter behavior or similarity score
Similarity in dense triads	$\sum_{j,h} ((1 - |z_i - z_j|) + (1 - |z_i - z_h|)) \cdot I(y_{ij} + y_{ji} + y_{ih} + y_{hi} + y_{hj} \geq 5)$	Indegree, outdegree, alter behavior or similarity score

Table 5.5 Common terms for SAOM behavioral function. y is a network tie, and z is the behavioral dependent variable.

The alter similarity and behavior scores are common specifications for modeling network influence. These statistics either sum or average over the behaviors of i's connections. The subtle distinction between the alter similarity and behavior scores is that the behavior scores model only the alters' behaviors, while similarity scores measure the distance between ego's and alters behaviors. The alter behavior scores may be more reasonable when modeling the adoption of innovations or diffusion of disease, where exposure is the most important determinant of behavioral change. The alter similarity scores may be more reasonable when modeling peer pressure or status-based adoptions, where changes in a behavioral state are primarily driven by a desire to fit in or "match" peer behavior.

Also of note in Table 5.5 are the endogenous network statistics. Coevolution models allow us to compute statistics not only on the *composition* of ego networks but also on the *structure* of the network. We can model change in behavioral states as a function of actors' position in network structure, such as isolation or degree centrality. We can also model interactions between network composition and structure. For instance, the similarity in dense triads statistic in Table 5.5 allows researchers to examine whether actors are more likely to change their behavioral state to match their peers' behavioral state when ego is embedded in a large number of dense triads with alters who share a behavioral state.

Example 5.2. A Coevolution Influence Model of Adolescent Drinking Behavior

We can now return to the example of peer influence on smoking behavior using a coevolution model to examine the Teenage Lifestyle Study network data. For this example, we'll be relying primarily on the RSiena package. Since many of the idiosyncrasies of the packages were discussed in detail in Chapter 3, the discussion here will focus primarily on preparing data for the behavioral function. Readers unfamiliar with RSiena may find it helpful to revisit the example in Chapter 3. Code to replicate this example is provided in the Chapter 5 supplement.

Data Preparation

As in the network-only SAOM, we begin by declaring our network as a dependent variable. Here, our network is provided as an array of three adjacency matrices. But, before we can include independent variables, now we have to specify our *behavioral* dependent variable in addition to our network dependent variable. RSiena requires that we provide these data as a matrix object with one column for each time period. We'll provide the dependent variable using sienaDependent command.

Next we'll define our independent variables. For this example, we have only the exogenous alcohol consumption covariate to declare. Once we've included the alcohol consumption variable, we compile our siena object. Our specification is similar to before, but now we have to specify two distinct dependent variables in our data set. Here, we use the following code:

>sienaDataCreate(Network=TLSnet, Behavior=TLSbeh, Alcohol).

This codes tells RSiena that we have two dependent variables, one called "Network" containing the time-varying network panels and one called "Behavior" containing the time-varying smoking behavior. We've also included alcohol consumption as an independent variable.

Before we can specify the algorithm and estimate the model, we also have to include effects into the model that tell RSiena what statistics to compute on the endogenously evolving network state. We can see what effects are available for the behavior and network functions using the effectsDocumentation command.

We'll start by including an exogenous alcohol consumption variable. We can also include endogenous statistics computed on the evolving behavioral and network states. We'll include the *total similarity* of ego's and alters' smoking behavior. This statistic is the summation over the difference between ego's smoking behavior and alters' smoking behavior. Higher values mean that actors' own smoking behavior would align more closely with alters' smoking behavior *if* the actor chooses to change their smoking behavior. This is our focal measure of network influence. We could also compute the value as an average over alters' smoking behavior instead of a sum, but since we're working with a small network, the mean is more sensitive to change in ego network size. We'll also include an isolates parameter to account for the possibility that network isolates smoke more or less than nonisolated actors.

Now that our behavioral function is specified, we have to specify our network function. We'll include sender, receiver, and absolute difference effects for alcohol consumption. We'll also include indegree popularity, reciprocity, and transitive triads as endogenous network statistics. The last thing that we have to include is the *smoking* effects on network change. This provides us with the "selection" component of our coevolution model. To do so, we'll include sender, receiver, and homophily effects for the network function.

Note here that coevolution models are prone to overspecification. The simultaneous evolution formulation can often induce collinearity and lead to models that are either hard to estimate or have extremely large variance estimates. In practice, it helps to start with simple models and to slowly introduce more complex specifications. Now that our model is specified, all we have to do is run it. Details on how to specify parameters for RSiena estimation are available in Chapter 3.

Analysis

Table 5.6 presents results from our coevolution model. Results are presented in two panels, one for the network change process and the other for the behavioral change process. We'll start by examining selection effects in the network function. The outdegree parameter is small, indicating that the probability that an actor will forge an outgoing tie when all other covariates are at 0 is low. The alcohol sender and receiver effects are insignificant, meaning that there is little evidence of a preference to become friends with alters who drink more frequently or for actors who drink more frequently to send more outgoing ties. However, the absolute difference coefficient is negative and significant, indicating a preference for peers to befriend alters who have similar levels of alcohol consumption.

Turning to endogenous network effects, the reciprocity parameter indicates that students have 9.69 times higher odds ($exp(2.271) = 9.69$) of nominating another student as a friend if the other student has already nominated a focal student as a friend. Similarly, the odds that an actor will nominate another student as a friend are about 3.5 times greater if the tie closes a transitive triplet ($exp(1.24) = 3.46$). The indegree popularity parameter is negative, indicating that increases in indegree centrality are associated with decreases in outgoing ties.

The final component of the network function is the endogenous smoking behavior effect. The sender, receiver, and homophily smoking effects are all insignificant. What this means is that smoking behavior is not contributing to network change; there is no evidence that actors prefer alters who smoke, that actors have similar smoking behavior, or that actors who do smoke are any more or less likely to create outgoing friendship ties. The insignificance of smoking homophily suggests that the network autocorrelation in smoking behavior is due to influence, since we found little evidence that actors select into networks with similar smoking behavior.

We can evaluate the scope of influence effects explicitly by turning to the behavior function. The "linear shape" parameter is the equivalent of the intercept in this model. It measures the trend between waves. Here, the parameter is insignificant, meaning that there is no systematic tendency for students to either increase or decrease their smoking behavior between waves. The isolates parameter is insignificant, indicating that network isolates are no more or less likely to change their smoking behavior at a given

	1. Coevolution SAOM
Network function	
Outdegree	−2.36*** (.312)
Smoking behavior	
Receiver	.306 (.388)
Sender	.095 (.337)
Same	.242 (.300)
Alcohol consumption	
Receiver	−.065 (.109)
Sender	.035 (.101)
Absolute difference	−.158* (.084)
Reciprocity	2.271*** (.198)
Transitive triad	1.24*** (.147)
Indegree popularity	−.142* (.066)
Behavior function	
Linear shape	.059 (.600)
Total smoking similarity	.722* (.346)
Alcohol consumption	.574 (.331)
Isolate	−.723 (3.05)

Table 5.6 Coevolution SAOM of change in networks and smoking behavior in the Teenage Lifestyle Study.[a] Coefficients and standard errors reported. Models estimated using method of moments.

[a]Rate parameters are omitted from table.
*$p < .05$. ***$p < .001$.

micro-step. The alcohol consumption parameter is also insignificant, although the p value for this parameter is .08.

Turning to influence effects, the coefficient for total smoking similarity is .722. This tells us that there is a preference for ego to change their smoking behavior to align with alters' smoking behavior. More precisely, imagine that ego has three friends. If all three friends were smokers and ego is not a smoker, the total similarity statistic would take a value of 3. Hence, in this hypothetical example, we could conclude that the total similarity statistic increases the odds that ego will pick up smoking by a factor of almost 9 ($exp(3 \cdot 0.722) = 8.72$). From this coefficient, we could conclude evidence of assimilation-based influence processes driven by a desire for students to "match" the smoking behaviors of their peers.

Model Checking

The first step in model checking is evaluating whether our stochastic approximation algorithm has converged. Parameter t ratios are all between $-.1$ and $.1$, and the model t ratio is $.25$. We can therefore conclude that the approximation algorithm has converged. The second thing that we have to do is assess goodness of fit. The procedures for assessing goodness of fit are identical to the network-evolution-only SAOM, but now we also record the number of predicted smokers in each simulated network and compare the metric to the observed number of smokers. Figure 5.1 presents goodness-of-fit results. The indegree and outdegree distributions are both excellent fits, with insignificant p values testing the difference between the observed and simulated statistics. The comparison for triad statistics is significant, but visual inspection of the triad census reveals that the model is performing quite well. Finally, the goodness-of-fit statistic for the behavioral distribution is an excellent fit with an insignificant test of the difference between the observed and simulated statistics. From this assessment, we can conclude that we have a very well-fitting model.

Another consideration is whether there are any extraneous parameters. Since coevolution models are usually underpowered (Stadfeld et al., 2020), we often have to exclude terms that might be theoretically relevant to improve convergence. We may also want to exclude unnecessary model terms to make room for more interesting ones. We can test whether insignificant model terms jointly improve model fit using Schweinberger's (2012) method. A joint test of the isolate effect and alcohol consumption effect is insignificant ($\chi^2 = 3.00, p = .22$), meaning that we could exclude these effects from our model without sacrificing model fit.

Finally, we'll check for time heterogeneity. The joint time heterogeneity test is insignificant ($\chi^2 = 13.57, p = .48$). Impressively, so are the time heterogeneity tests for *every* parameter. We can therefore conclude (quite confidently) that time heterogeneity is not influencing our coevolution model.

Advanced Interpretation

Since we're working within a SAOM framework, we need to use special procedures to interpret the effects of interactions in both the behavior and influence models. It's most useful to conduct this type of assessment using predicted values. Figure 5.2 presents the predicted odds of tie formation and behavioral change as a function of smoking homophily. Consistent with primary results, the effect of peer smoking behavior is much more pronounced in the behavioral function. The odds that a student will transition to a smoker from a nonsmoker double when alters are smokers. The smoking behavior

116

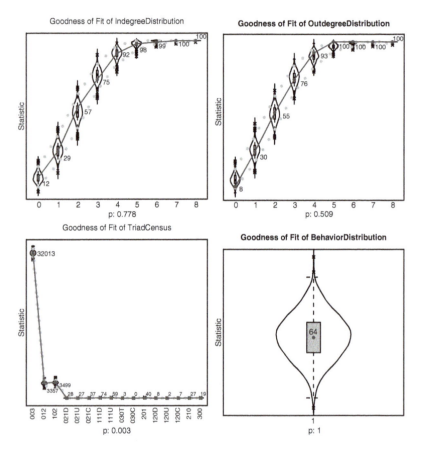

Figure 5.1 Goodness of fit for SAOM. Violin plots report interquartile range for simulated statistics of target network and behavioral state (here, Wave 3 Teenage Lifestyle Study). Solid dots and lines report observed statistics of the target network or count of smoking students. The *p* value tests the null hypothesis that the simulated and observed distributions are equal.

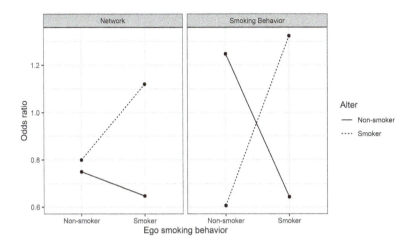

Figure 5.2   Predicted odds of tie formation and behavioral change by smoking behavior. All controls held at 0.

plot also reveals that the peer influence effects are equally strong for both smoking and nonsmoking behavior.

The panel for the network function reveals heterogeneity between smokers and nonsmokers in their preferences for peers. While nonsmokers do not appear to have a large preference for peers based on their smoking behaviors, smokers have a large preference for other smokers. This suggests that selection on smoking behavior may be influential for smokers but not for nonsmokers, although, again, the smoking effects in the network function are insignificant.

Since the behavioral function is a nonlinear probability model, we can't compare coefficients between different models fit to the same data. We can, however, use the procedures discussed in Chapter 3 to draw cross-model comparisons. Recall that this involves first calculating conditional predicted values and then calculating the difference in conditional predicted values after model specification has changed.

Missing Data

Because we are within the SAOM framework, we are able to impute missing behavioral data for SAOM using the procedures described in Chapter 3. These procedures may include univariate imputation or multiple imputation.

However, listwise deletion is generally inappropriate, and so imputation on
the dependent variable is *preferred* to deleting missing observations. This
is for two reasons. First, like standard SAOM, network statistics are altered
by deleting actors with missing data. Second, because we regard the behavioral dependent variable as endogenous, listwise deletion will also alter the
values of endogenous behavioral statistics, such as peer influence measures.
Since the coevolution model is a multivariate model for simultaneous network and behavioral change, deleting a single actor can bias the coefficients
for selection *and* influence processes.

An Alternative Approach: Simulating Network Diffusion

A final possible approach for analyzing influence processes is to use network
simulation. Network simulations entail a broad range of tools for examining
the rate at which a contagion travels through a social network. Simulation
models are common within studies of health behavior and disease (adams
& Schaefer, 2016) and the adoption of behaviors, attitudes, and innovations
(Centola & Macy, 2006; Valente, 1995). Simulation methods generally entail
specifying a time-varying network structure (either empirically or synthet-
ically) and then specifying an adoption threshold, such as the number of
connections that share an attribute required to change a behavior. If a node
crosses that threshold, then their behavior changes. The model then iterates
in a sequence until the network has been saturated. The model provides a
simulated data set that can be analyzed to determine what network characteristics influence the rate at which a signal spreads.

More complicated models are available that incorporate statistical frameworks (Jenness, Goodreau, & Morris, 2018; Snijders & Steglich, 2015),
build on epidemiologic models (Jenness et al., 2018), and specify more
intricate adoption thresholds (Berry, Cameron, Park, & Macy, 2019). One
characterizing feature of most simulation methods is that they require a prespecified set of parameters dictating how quickly an exposed actor adopts a
contagion. If researchers are interested in examining the rate of network diffusion and/or examining how network structure or composition can increase
or slow the speed of diffusion, simulation models are a powerful tool.

Since many of these models are mathematical rather than statistical, they
will not be reviewed in depth here. Applied examples of diffusion models
can be found in Centola and Macy (2006), Macy (1991), or Watts (2002).
Simulation methods can also be integrated with coevolution models or
TERGM to simulate coevolution of network and behavior change. Readers interested in this approach can consult Snijders and Steglich (2015) or

Jenness et al. (2018). An applied example of a study integrating coevolution models with diffusion simulation can be found in adams and Schaefer (2016).

How Should We Think About Network Influence?

TNAM and SAOM are the dominant longitudinal models for studying network influence. But results often differ between models. In TNAM, alcohol use was the most robust predictor of smoking behavior. In SAOM, it was insignificant. Our choice of model may change substantive conclusions and alter how we interpret statistical results. So, which model should you use?

The most important limitation of TNAM for this type of inference is that the model does not distinguish selection from influence. We have to determine whether network autocorrelation is caused by influence processes on theoretical grounds or using an instrument. In contrast, SAOM has explicit procedures for disentangling selection and influence effects. But this strength comes with the weakness that SAOM relies on much more stringent assumptions than TNAM. SAOM is inappropriate for network and behavioral processes that are not agent driven. This is particularly important to emphasize for coevolution models, since some actor-level attributes are not under actors' control, such as victimization from violent crime. In these cases, SAOM cannot be used to study influence effects.

Similarly, SAOM makes strong assumptions on the timing of behavioral and network change. If ties form simultaneously (such as in bilateral trade agreements), behaviors change simultaneously (two friends decide to sign up for a gym membership together), or ties and behaviors change simultaneously (I meet a new friend when I start going to the gym), SAOM will misrepresent the change process. Regardless of any strengths, coevolution model results are uninformative if these assumptions are not met.

A final key distinction between SAOM and TNAM is that SAOM accounts for unobserved change processes, while TNAM does not. In this regard, TNAM is similar to TERGM in that it implicitly assumes that the network structure at the time of observation is representative of the network structure at the time that a behavior was changed. SAOM, in contrast, imputes the unmeasured sequencing of events. If network structure changes rapidly or there are long time windows between network panels, TNAM will likely perform worse than SAOM.

Researchers may find the following guidance helpful in choosing whether to use a SAOM or TNAM to study network influence. The first question a researcher should ask is: "Am I interested in network influence, or only examining network effects?" If the answer is "I am interested in network influence," SAOM will likely be preferable, as it more explicitly deals with the conflation of selection and influence. In contrast, if the answer is "I am only interested in controlling for network dependencies, examining network effects, or interpreting the correlation between ego and alter attributes," then either model will work.

The second question a researcher should ask is whether SAOM assumptions are appropriate for their data. Coevolution models require (1) that *both* behavioral and network change are agent driven, (2) that *both* behavioral and network change are sequentially ordered (no simultaneous changes), and (3) that behavioral change is a *discrete* occurrence, rather than a gradual shift. If these assumptions cannot be met, SAOM is inappropriate. Even if researchers are primarily concerned with distinguishing selection from influence, SAOM fails to represent either of these processes if the assumptions of the model are violated by the data at hand. In these cases, researchers should prefer TNAM and think about other possible solutions to dealing with the problem of selection and influence (such as an instrument).

The third question a researcher should ask is whether there are long time periods between network panels and whether ties or behaviors can be expected to change rapidly. If there are large gaps between panel data collection and/or ties and behaviors change rapidly, SAOM will be more appropriate, as TNAM uses no procedures for dealing with unmeasured tie changes.

A Brief Tangent: Always Test for Network Autocorrelation When Examining Data Sampled From a Complete Network

A final point to make regards the prevalence of network autocorrelation in studies that *are not* interested in network processes. Sometimes researchers fit generic panel models to longitudinal data that are sampled from complete networks without controlling for network autocorrelation. The decision, when justified, is typically defended on the grounds that the model does not include any network statistics. This is common, for instance, in studies using Waves I and II of the saturated AddHealth sample, where data on complete school networks are collected, but researchers often study the panels without including network statistics. Such data are not randomly sampled. Students who go to the same school may be similar on a number of attributes for unobserved reasons. Hence, a generic panel model will usually give downward biased standard errors and may bias coefficients if the cause of network autocorrelation is not controlled (Shalizi & Thomas, 2011; Young, 2014).

Researchers must account for the possibility of network autocorrelation when studying panel data sampled from a complete network. Researchers can evaluate network autocorrelation by comparing the fit of TNAM to a generic panel model or by calculating Moran's I on each wave of panel data. In cases where network autocorrelation is detected, TNAM should be used as the preferred modeling strategy. Even though the interest is not to analyze network processes in these circumstances, TNAM allows for similarities between students that may influence standard errors and coefficients for independent variables of interest if left uncontrolled.

Conclusion

TNAM and SAOM provide strategies for examining network influence. TNAM is able to model the network autocorrelation in a behavioral response variable and offers a flexible modeling framework that can be generically applied to network panel data. However, the model is unable to disentangle selection and influence. Coevolution models allow researchers to disentangle selection from influence but make more stringent assumptions on the causes of behavioral change and the sequencing of unobserved network and behavioral change. When SAOM assumptions are tenable, the strengths of the coevolution model allow for much more precise and often theoretically informative inference. TNAM, by contrast, can be applied in a range of settings where SAOM assumptions are violated or in contexts where researchers are not explicitly interested in distinguishing selection from influence.

Technical reading on TNAM can be found in Doreian (1981), Leenders (2002), or Mizruchi and Neuman (2008). Applied examples of TNAM can be found in Tita and Radil (2011), McPherson and Nieswiadomy (2005), Kalenkoski and Lacombe (2008), Mizruchi and Stearns (2006), Papachristos and Bastomski (2018), and Gimpel and Schuknecht (2003). Further guidance on implementing coevolution models can be found in Ripley et al. (2020). A technical discussion is available in Steglich et al. (2010). Applied examples of coevolution models can be found in Turanovic and Young (2016), Haynie et al. (2014), Ragan et al. (2014), Weerman (2011), Duxbury and Haynie (2020b), adams and Schaefer (2016), Schaefer (2018), or Lewis and Kaufman (2018).

CHAPTER 6. CONCLUSION

Longitudinal network models entail a range of powerful methods for analyzing network dynamics and behavioral change. At the same time, as a rapidly developing area, many of the tools, methods, and diagnostics described in this text will most likely change in the coming years. Indeed, between 2000 and 2010, the standards for publishing a network analysis in a reputable scientific journal shifted from descriptions of summary statistics and network structure to requiring some type of inferential approach. This chapter looks ahead to areas where there is growing activity and lingering questions. Practitioners should keep an eye to these areas of research to stay abreast of the most recent methods.

Missing Data

Perhaps one of the most important areas for methodological development is missing data. Missing data present a challenge for network analysis because listwise deletion is usually inappropriate, even if data are missing on the dependent variable. Since data are nonindependent, standard imputation strategies can only be used in special cases for exogenous attributes. Moreover, model-based and Bayesian imputation strategies rely on the strength of the model for missing tie data (Koskinen et al., 2013; Robins et al., 2004). When this model is misspecified, imputations suffer.

The upside is that statistical network models tend to be robust to modest amounts of missingness (Borgatti et al., 2006; Kossinets, 2006). Empirical assessments also demonstrate that model-based imputations generally outperform listwise deletion of missing data, both in terms of statistical estimates from models fit to imputed data (Hipp et al., 2015; Koskinen et al., 2013; Krause, Huisman, & Snijders, 2018; Krause, Huisman, Steglich, & Snijders, 2018), as well as in terms of recovering network structure (Smith & Moody, 2013; Smith et al., 2017).

As methods for missing network data continue to develop in the coming years, the state of the art is likely to change as methodologists gain a better sense of how to improve upon current model-based imputation strategies. Until then, as a general rule, researchers should use some type of imputation strategy in the presence of missing data. If data are only missing on exogenous attributes in small amounts, then even univariate imputations will generally be sufficient. However, if there is more than about 10% missing tie data, researchers will need to consider a more complex model-based imputation strategy. Whatever strategy is used, researchers should assess the sensitivity of results to different imputation strategies and model specifications to ensure that their primary findings are not an artifact of a misspecified imputation model or an improper imputation strategy.

Measurement Error

As scholars are collecting more and more network data, a growing body of literature has developed examining measurement error. To conceptualize how measurement error arises, consider a classical example. Granovetter (1973) famously argued that between-group connections in social networks facilitate access to unique resources and information. So, what is a social network in this context? A friendship? A kinship? A romantic partnership? An acquaintanceship? A coworker? Or will a simple phone call suffice? In many theoretical conceptualizations, social ties are regarded as encompassing some conglomerate of "all of the above." However, in practice, we usually only have information on a single type of tie.

In cases where we are conceptualizing social networks as containing multiple dimensions of relations but we are only able to measure a single dimension (e.g., a friendship), we encounter well-known problems related to construct validity: Our measurement only partially captures the underlying construct that we would like to measure. Consequently, our measurements have some error. If the error is random, then the only consequence is conservative coefficients. However, if there is systematic error, the bias in coefficients can either understate or exaggerate a relationship or provide the incorrect sign. Thus, as in classical regression, the principal threat to inference is systematic measurement error.

In addition to questions of construct validity, researchers are increasingly concerned with the accuracy of peer reports (An & Schramski, 2015). In the context of network surveys, for example, perceptions of friendship may differ between individuals. i may nominate j as a friend, but j may disagree. In this case, our measure of "friendship" is in fact a measure of friendship *perceptions*, which we take to be a proxy for friendship.

A growing body of research examines these issues, leveraging myriad strategies to grapple with construct validity and respondent reporting error. Lee and Butts (2018), for instance, examine three empirical networks, finding that examining only *reciprocated* ties in friendship networks does a better job of recapturing the "true" friendship network structure than relying on peer reports alone. An (2022) similarly shows that incorporating information on multiple peer reports helps to smooth over response error in friendship networks and that, in some contexts, the measurement error in peer reports can be estimated with regression. Still other scholars have begun to consider how to recover latent networks from multiple relational measures (Kim, Lee, Xue, & Xiaoyue, 2018). Researchers should keep an eye to this developing literature to address construct validity and measurement error in their own work.

Interpretation

Another growing area in statistical network analysis is interpretation. Scholars have increasingly drawn attention to how current interpretations for complex relational measures are inaccurate (Duxbury, 2021c; Snijders & Lomi, 2019; Stewart, Schweinberger, Bojanowski, & Morris, 2019). Recent methods have been proposed by Snijders and Lomi (2019) and Duxbury (2021c) for handling these issues in the context of exogenous interactions. However, the problem still persists in the context of endogenous network effects.

Network measures are complex interactions. A triad cannot form without creating at least two additional two-stars and influencing the degree distribution. Hence, current recommendations that parameters for endogenous network effects can be interpreted as "increasing the odds of a tie change given a one-unit increase in structural measure, holding all else constant" are usually misleading. We cannot, except in special cases of lowest-order network statistics (like degree centrality), hold one network measure constant while increasing the value of another network measure.

Until these issues have been sorted out, researchers may benefit from the following guidance. Issues related to interpreting endogenous network effects only arise in models that include multiple network effects. Imagine that we have fit a model including two-stars, degree centrality, and triadic closure, only to find that the two-stars and degree centrality parameters are insignificant and worsen model fit as compared to a model that only includes triadic closure. We could therefore safely exclude two-stars and degree centrality. In this case, triadic closure is the only remaining endogenous network statistic, and the average marginal effect of triadic closure can be interpreted as it would for any other variable. Further, in the case where we only include *two* endogenous network measures, we have a two-way interaction that can be interpreted using the average marginal effect framework or predicted values, as described in prior chapters.

In more complicated situations where there are *at least three* network statistics included into a model, predicted values are currently the most promising method for interpretation. This strategy is illustrated in Chapters 3 and 5 for SAOM, where predictions are generated at each level of an interaction. These results can be presented graphically or using tables. Since this method relies only on predictions, it is straightforward to apply to REM, TERGM, and TNAM as well.

Causal Inference

Analysts examining generative processes of network structure are often interested in recovering a causal relationship from observational network data (An, Beauvile, & Rosche, 2022). Yet, statistical network models pose important problems for drawing causal inference due to interdependence and high collinearity. For example, consider an instrumental variable design. Instrumental variable regression consistently estimates the causal effect of a variable when two conditions are met. First, the instrument must be relevant—that is, it must be closely correlated with the independent variable of interest. Second, the instrument must *not* correlate with the outcome *other* than through its association with the endogenous variable.

Now consider applying these two conditions in an analysis using SAOM where we are interested in the causal effect of transitive triplets on tie formation. Given that network structures are usually highly correlated (Duxbury, 2021a), it would be difficult to find an instrument that correlates only with transitive triplets *and not* any other network measure without encountering problems related to weak instruments. Moreover, because transitive triplets represent a particular tie configuration, we would also require that the instrument is correlated with transitive triplets but *not* tie formation in general. Thus, to instrument transitive triplets, we would have to find a variable that is uncorrelated with any other type of triad or network ties themselves. These conditions mean that finding a valid instrument for network effects can often be extremely difficult.

Prior studies have generally used two strategies to evaluate causal network effects. The first is network experiments. Using online platforms, scholars can randomly assign individuals to network positions such that they can experimentally manipulate network structure and estimate its causal effect (Centola, 2010; Melamed et al., 2018). A famous example comes from Centola (2010), who experimentally assigns individuals within an online community to interact with other individuals who have varying levels of physical activity. Because node position is experimentally assigned, it is impossible for actors to select into distinct positions. The estimated effect of peer health behavior on ego health behavior must be causal.

A second approach is to create instrumental variables for peer effects, usually using peer background characteristics or creating novel instruments during collection. For example, O'Malley, Elwert, Rosenquist, Zaslavsky, and Christakis (2014) use genetic alleles as instruments to estimate peer effects on weight status. An (2015a) similarly shows how peer effect instruments can be gathered with survey administration, creating an instrument for peer smoking behavior by compiling a battery of measures on a peer's home context (parental attitudes to smoking; parental, sibling, and relative smoking status; whether cigarettes are stored at home; and distance to the nearest cigarette store).

Models for Relational Event Data

An emerging area of methodological development is modeling relational event data. Before Butts's (2008) seminal work, this area was largely overlooked. However, the increased availability of fine-grained relational event data from administrative records, digital traces, and geotagged records has contributed to enthusiasm for models for relational event data analysis (Kitts, 2014). Recently, scholars have expanded on Butts's (2008) original work to provide an actor-oriented framework (Stadtfeld & Block, 2017), to account for unobserved heterogeneity (DuBois et al., 2013), and to include multilevel and bipartite networks (Brandenberger, 2018; Lerner, Lomi, Mowbray, Rollings, & Tranmer, 2017). Other rapidly developing areas include goodness-of-fit assessments (Brandenberger, 2019) and evaluations of model robustness (Duxbury, n.d.; Lerner & Lomi, 2020a). Researchers interested in modeling relational event data should keep an eye to the most recent model extensions and diagnostics.

Unobserved Heterogeneity in Network Panel Models

Unobserved heterogeneity is a major issue in network panel analysis. Node-level measures for key variables often suffer from measurement error or go unaccounted for during data collection (Box-Steffensmeier et al., 2018). Models that allow for hierarchical structure and node-level random effects are available to both SAOM and TERGM, but they are currently only implemented as Bayesian models (Koskinen & Snijders, 2007; Schweinberger, 2020; Schweinberger & Handcock, 2015; Thiemichen et al., 2016). A frequentist version of TERGM that controls for unmeasured node-level heterogeneity is available, but the method is limited in that it only estimates pseudolikelihood (Box-Steffensmeier et al., 2018; van Duijn, Snijders, & Zijlstra,

2004). While empirical comparisons suggest that this "frailty ERGM" provides more conservative variance estimates than conventional ERGM (Box-Steffensmeier, Campbell, Christenson, & Morgan, 2019), pseudolikelihood is usually unreliable and only consistently estimates the maximum likelihood estimates in extremely large data sets (Strauss & Ikeda, 1990).[1]

It seems inevitable that many of the models developed for Bayesian estimation will eventually be available within a frequentist framework. Until such models become available, researchers concerned with unobserved heterogeneity may find it useful to consult one of these Bayesian strategies or the frailty TERGM. Researchers concerned with unobserved heterogeneity and who want to stay within a frequentist framework can also include a vector of node-level indicator variables. This will eliminate any node-level unobserved heterogeneity but also will prevent researchers from including time-invariant node-level measures.

Scalability

A perennial area of activity is scalable estimation. Large-scale network panel data can be prohibitive for estimating many network models. The estimation frameworks for TERGM and SAOM, especially, are computationally expensive even for modestly sized data sets that include roughly 1,000 actors or that contain more three waves of data. Prior studies have outlined several strategies for scaling network models to larger data sets. Most of these strategies are specific to each model. For example, an interesting property of TERGM is that the bias in pseudolikelihood estimates declines as network size increases (An, 2016; Cranmer et al., 2021; Strauss & Ikeda, 1990). This means that if we have large network data—usually in the tens of thousands of nodes—we can estimate TERGM as a logistic regression and obtain accurate results.

In SAOM, we are able to scale the model to larger data by dividing the network into local subsets. This "divide-and-conquer" approach relies on the reasoning that, in large networks, actors do not have global knowledge on all possible alters but are aware of actors in their local neighborhood. If we have a measure of local subgroups either through preassigned categories (e.g., students attending the same schools, employees working in the same department) or are able to detect local subgroups, such as using a community

---

[1] These consistency results are also only available for conventional pseudolikelihood estimation and have not been proven for the restricted pseudolikelihood estimation used in frailty ERGM.

128

detection algorithm, we may be able to estimate individual models to each subset and then pool the estimates for final presentation. Note, however, that this approach will necessarily sacrifice any ties that span distinct subgroups. It may be less appropriate in studies where cross-group ties are of interest or are empirically common.

In addition to these strategies, a growing body of literature focuses on creating scalable MCMC estimation algorithms for network data. Computational statisticians have dedicated significant effort to developing more efficient estimation algorithms, some specifically for statistical network models (Caimo & Friel, 2011; Krivitsky, 2017; Stivala, Garry, & Lomi, 2020). For example, Krivitsky (2017) demonstrates how contrastive divergence—a type of unsupervised machine learning—can be used to find reasonable approximates of the maximum likelihood to initiate MCMC maximum likelihood estimation in ERGM, reducing estimation times for large networks or complicated models. Many of these options are incorporated into current software. For instance, the btergm, tergm, and RSiena software packages all provide utilities to tune estimation algorithms. Researchers working with large network data and encountering issues related to estimating their models should brush up on the most recent developments in estimating large network models and change their estimation algorithm to match the current state of the art.

Conclusion

The suite of available tools for handling missing data, diagnostics, estimation, and interpretation in longitudinal network models is likely to grow in the coming years. Longitudinal network analysis has reached a point of maturity where the models that we use today may change in terms of specification, estimation, or frameworks for diagnostics, but we are unlikely to derive many more new modeling frameworks that overhaul our current tools, at least not in the near future. However, our *strategies* for expanding, specifying, estimating, diagnosing, and interpreting results from longitudinal network models are still in flux. As researchers become increasingly proficient in applying the range of models described in this book, it will be necessary to monitor the methodological literature to handle each of these developing issues.

REFERENCES

adams, j. (2019). *Gathering social network data*. Los Angeles, CA.

adams, j., & Schaefer, D. R. (2016). How initial prevalence moderates network-based smoking change: Estimating contextual effects with stochastic actor-based models. *Journal of Health and Social Behavior*, *57*(1), 22–38.

Albert, R., Jeong, H., & Barabasi, A.-L. (1999). Diameter of the world-wide web. *Nature*, *401*, 130–131.

Allison, P. D. (1999). Comparing logit and probit coefficients across groups. *Sociological Methods and Research*, *28*(2), 186–208.

Almquist, Z., & Butts, C. T. (2013). Dynamic network logistic regression: A logistic choice analysis of inter- and intra-group blog citation dynamics in the 2004 US presidential election. *Political Analysis*, *21*, 430–448.

Almquist, Z., & Butts, C. T. (2014). Logistic network regression for scalable analysis of networks with joint edge/vertex dynamics. *Sociological Methodology*, *44*, 273–321.

Amati, V., Schonenberger, F., & Snijders, T. A. B. (2015). Estimation of Stochastic Actor-oriented Models for the Evolution of Networks by Generalized Method of Moments. *Journal de la Societe Francaise de Statistique*, *156*(1), 140–165.

An, W. (2015a). Instrumental variables estimates of peer effects in social networks. *Social Science Research*, *50*, 382–394.

An, W. (2015b). Multilevel meta network analysis with application to study network dynamics of network interventions. *Social Networks*, *43*(1), 48–56.

An, W. (2016). Fitting ERGMs on big networks. *Social Science Research*, *59*(1), 107–119.

An, W. (2022). You said, they said: A framework on informant accuracy with application to studying self-reports and peer reports. *Social Networks*, *70*, 187–197.

An, W., Beauvile, R., & Rosche, B. (2022). Causal network analysis. *Annual Review of Sociology*, *48*, 15–35.

An, W., & Schramski, S. (2015). Analysis of contested reports in exchange networks based on actors' credibility. *Social Networks*, *40*, 25–33.

Anselin, L. (2001). Rao's score test in spatial econometrics. *Journal of Statistical Planning and Inference*, *97*(1), 113–139.

Berry, G., Cameron, C. J., Park, P., & Macy, M. (2019). The opacity problem in social contagion. *Social Networks*, *56*(1), 93–101.

Besag, J. E. (1972). Nearest-neighbour systems and the auto-logistic model for binary data. *Journal of the Royal Statistical Society Series B*, *34*(1), 75–83.

Besag, J. E. (1974). Spatial interaction and the statistical analysis of lattice systems. *Journal of the Royal Statistical Society Series B*, *36*(2), 192–236.

Block, P. (2015). Reciprocity, transitivity, and the mysterious three-cycle. *Social Networks*, *40*, 163–173.

Block, P., Koskinen, J., Holloway, J., Steglich, C., & Stadtfeld, C. (2018) Change we can believe in: Comparing longitudinal network models on consistency, interpretability, and predictive power. *Social Networks*, *52*, 180–191. (DOI:10.1016/j.socnet.2017.08.001)

Block, P., Stadtfeld, C., & Snijders, T. A. B. (2019). Forms of dependence: Comparing SAOMs and ERGMs from basic principles. *Sociological Methods & Research*, *48*(1), 202–239.

Bollen, K. A., & Brand, J. E. (2010). A general panel model with random and fixed effects: A structural equations approach. *Social Forces*, *89*(1), 1–34.

130

Borgatti, S. P., Carley, K. M., & Krackhardt, D. (2006). On the robustness of centrality measures under conditions of imperfect data. *Social Networks, 28*(2), 124–136.

Box-Steffensmeier, J. M., Campbell, B. W., Christenson, D. P., & Morgan, J. W. (2019). Substantive implications of unobserved heterogeneity: Testing the frailty approach to exponential random graph models. *Social Networks, 59*(1), 141–153.

Box-Steffensmeier, J. M., Christenson, D. P., & Morgan, J. W. (2018). Modeling unobserved heterogeneity in social networks with the frailty exponential random graph model. *Political Analysis, 26*(1), 3–19.

Brandenberger, L. (2018). Trading favors—examining the temporal dynamics of reciprocity in congressional collaborations using relational event models. *Social Networks, 54*, 238–253.

Brandenberger, L. (2019). Predicting network events to assess goodness of fit of relational event models. *Political Analysis, 27*, 556–571.

Breen, R., Karlson, K. B., & Holm, A. (2018). Interpreting and understanding logits, probits, and other nonlinear probability models. *Annual Review of Sociology, 44*, 39–54.

Butts, C. T. (2008). A relational event framework for social action. *Sociological Methodology, 38*(1), 155–200.

Butts, C. T. (2009). Revisiting the foundations of network analysis. *Science, 24*, 414–216.

Butts, C. T. (2017). Comment: Actor orientation and relational event models. *Sociological Methodology, 47*, 47–56.

Butts, C. T., & Marcum, C. (2017). A relational event approach to modeling behavioral dynamics. In A. Pilny & M. S. Poole (Eds.), *Group processes: Data-drive computational approaches* (pp. 51–92). Cham, Switzerland: Springer International Publishing.

Caimo, A., & Friel, N. (2011). Bayesian inference for exponential random graph models. *Social Networks, 33*(1), 41–55.

Centola, D. (2010). The spread of behavior in an online social network experiment. *Science, 329*, 1194–1197.

Centola, D., & Macy, M. (2006). Complex contagions and the weakness of long ties. *American Journal of Sociology, 113*(3), 702–734.

Cham, H., Reshetnyak, E., Rosenfeld, B., & Breitbart, W. (2017). Full information maximum likelihood estimation for latent variable interactions with incomplete indicators. *Multivariate Behavioral Research, 52*(1), 12–30.

Coutinho, J. A., Diviak, T., Bright, D., & Koskinen, J. (2020). Multilevel determinants of collaboration between organised criminal groups. *Social Networks, 63*, 56–69.

Cranmer, S. J., Desmarais, B. A., & Menninga, E. J. (2012). Complex dependencies in the alliance network. *Conflict Management and Peace Studies, 29*(3), 279–313.

Cranmer, S. J., Desmarais, B. A., & Morgan, J. W. (2021). *Inferential network analysis.* Cambridge, MA: Cambridge University Press.

Cranmer, S. J., Heinrich, T., & Desmarais, B. A. (2014). Reciprocity and the structural determinants of the international sanctions network. *Social Networks, 36*(1), 5–22.

Cranmer, S. J., Leifeld, P., McClurg, S. D., & Rolfe, M. (2017). Navigating the range of statistical tools for inferential network analysis. *American Journal of Political Science, 61*(1), 237–251.

Desmarais, B. A., & Cranmer, S. J. (2012a). Micro-level interpretation of exponential random graph models with application to estuary networks. *Policy Studies Journal, 40*(1), 402–434.

Desmarais, B. A., & Cranmer, S. J. (2012b). Statistical inference for valued-edge networks: The generalized exponential random graph model. *PLoS One, 7*(1), 1–12.

Desmarais, B. A., & Cranmer, S. J. (2012c). Statistical mechanics of networks: Estimation and uncertainty. *Physica A: Statistical Mechanics and its Applications, 391*(4), 1865–1876.

Dittrich, D., Leenders, R., & Mulder, J. (2020). Network autocorrelation modeling: Bayesian techniques for estimating and testing multiple network autocorrelations. *Sociological Methodology*, *50*(1), 169–214.

Doreian, P. (1981). Estimating linear models with spatially distributed data. *Sociological Methodology*, *12*(1), 359–388.

Dow, M. M. (2007). Galton's problem as multiple network autocorrelation effects: Cultural train transmission and ecological constraint. *Cross Cultural research*, *41*(1), 336–363.

Dow, M. M., Burton, M. L., & White, D. R. (1982). Network autocorrelation: A simulation study of a foundational problem in regression and survey research. *Social Networks*, *4*(1), 169–200.

DuBois, C., Butts, C. T., & Smyth, P. (2013). Stochastic blockmodeling of relational event dynamics. *Proceedings of the 16th International Conference on Artificial Intelligence and Statistics*, *31*(1), 238–245.

Duxbury, S. (n.d.). *Left truncation in relational event models: Consequences and corrections for network parameter inference.*

Duxbury, S. (2021a). Diagnosing multicollinearity in exponential random graph models. *Sociological Methods and Research*, *50*(2), 491–530. (DOI: 10.1177/0049124118782543)

Duxbury, S. (2021b). A general panel model for unobserved time heterogeneity with application to the politics of mass incarceration. *Sociological Methodology*, *51*(2), 1–30.

Duxbury, S. (2021c). The problem of scaling in exponential random graph models. *Sociological Methods & Research*. (Advance online publication)

Duxbury, S., & Haynie, D. (2020b). School suspension and social selection: Labeling, network change, and adolescent academic achievement. *Social Science Research*, *85*(1), 1–16.

Duxbury, S., & Haynie, D. (2021a). Network embeddedness in illegal online markets: Endogenous sources of prices and profit in anonymous criminal drug trade. *Socio-economic Review*. (Advance online publication)

Duxbury, S., & Haynie, D. (2021b). Shining a light on the shadows: Endogenous trade structure and the growth of online illegal markets. *American Journal of Sociology*, *127*, 787—827.

Duxbury, S., & Haynie, D. L. (2020a). The responsivenss of criminal networks to intentional attacks: Disrupting darknet drug trafficking. *PLOS One*, *15*, e0238019.

Efron, B. (1974). The efficiency of Cox's likelihood function for censored data. *Journal of the American Statistical Association*, *72*, 557–565.

Elhorst, J. P., Lacombe, D. J., & Piras, G. (2012). On model specification and parameter space definitions in higher order spatial econometric models. *Regional Science and Urban Economics*, *42*(1), 211–220.

Frank, O., & Strauss, D. (1986). Markov graphs. *Journal of the American Statistical Association*, *81*(395), 832–842.

Fujimoto, K., Chou, C.-P., & Valente, T. W. (2011). The network autocorrelation model using two-mode data: Affiliation exposure and potential bias in the autocorrelation parameter. *Social Networks*, *33*(1), 231–243.

Geyer, C. J., & Thompson, E. A. (1992). Constrained Monte Carlo maximum likelihood for dependent data. *Journal of the Royal Statistical Society B*, *54*(3), 657–699.

Gimpel, J. G., & Schuknecht, J. E. (2003). Political participation and the accessibility of the ballot box. *Political Geography*, *22*(5), 471–488.

Goodreau, S. M., Kitts, J. A., & Morris, M. (2009). Birds of a feather, or friend of a friend? Using exponential random graph models to investigate adolescent social networks. *Demography*, *46*(1), 103–125.

Granovetter, M. (1973). The strength of weak ties. *American Journal of Sociology*, *78*(6), 347–367.

Granovetter, M. (1985). Economic action and social structure: The problem of embeddedness. *American Journal of Sociology, 91*, 481–510.

Handcock, M. S., Robins, G., Snijders, T. A. B., Moody, J., & Besag, J. (2003). Assessing degeneracy in statistical models of social networks. *Journal of the American Statistical Association, 76*(1), 33–50.

Hanneke, S., Fu, W., & Xing, E. P. (2010). Discrete temporal models of social networks. *Electronic Journal of Statistics, 4*, 585–605.

Haynie, D. L., Doogan, N. J., & Soller, B. (2014). Gender, friendship networks, and delinquency: A dynamic network approach. *Criminology, 52*(4), 688–722.

Hays, J. C., Kachi, A., & Franzes, R. J. J. (2010). A spatial model incorporating dynamic, endogenous network interdependence: A political science application. *Statistical Methodology, 7*(1), 406–428.

Hipp, J. R., Wang, C., Butts, C. T., Jose, R., & Lakon, C. M. (2015). Research note: The consequences of different methods for handling missing network data in stochastic actor based models. *Social Networks, 41*(1), 57–71.

Holland, P. W., & Leinhardt, S. (1971). Transitivty in structural models of small groups. *Small Group Research, 2*, 107–124.

Holland, P. W., & Leinhardt, S. (1981). An exponential family of probability distributions for directed graphs. *Journal of the American Statistical Association, 76*(373), 33–50.

Honaker, J., & King, G. (2010). What to do about missing values in time series cross-section data. *American Journal of Political Science, 54*(3), 561–581.

Huisman, M., & Snijders, T. A. B. (2003). Statistical analysis of longitudinal network data with changing composition. *Sociological Methods & Research, 32*, 253–287.

Huisman, M., & Steglich, C. (2008). Treatment of non-response in longitudinal network studies. *Social Networks, 30*(1), 297–308.

Hunter, D. R. (2007). Curved exponential family models for social networks. *Social Networks, 29*(2), 216–230.

Hunter, D. R., Handcock, M. S., Butts, C. T., Goodreau, S. M., & Morris, M. (2008). ERGM: A package to fit, simulate, and diagnose exponential-family random graph models. *Journal of Statistical Software, 24*(3), 1–29.

Ingold, K., & Leifeld, P. (2014). Structural and institutional determinants of influence reputation: A comparison of collaborative and adversarial policy networks in decision making and implementation. *Journal of Public Administration Research and Theory, 26*(1), 1–18.

Jenness, S. M., Goodreau, S. M., & Morris, M. (2018). Epimodel: An R package for mathematical modeling of infectious disease over networks. *Journal of Statistical Software, 84*(8), 1–42.

Kalenkoski, C. M., & Lacombe, D. J. (2008). Effects of minimum wage of youth employment: The importance of accounting for spatial autocorrelation. *Journal of Labor Research, 29*(4), 303–317.

Karlson, K. B., Holm, A., & Breen, R. (2012). Comparing regression coefficients between same-sample nested models using logit and probit: A new method. *Sociological Methodology, 42*(1), 286–313.

Kim, B., Lee, K. H., Xue, L., & Xiaoyue, N. (2018). A review of dynamic network models with latent variables. *Statistical Survey, 12*, 102–135.

Kitts, J. (2014). Beyond networks in structural theories of exchange: Promises from computational social science. *Advances in Group Processes, 31*, 263–298.

Kitts, J., Pallotti, F., Lomi, A., Quintane, E., & Mascia, D. (2017). Investigating the temporal dynamics of interorganizational exchange: Patient transfers among italian hospitals. *American Journal of Sociology, 123*(3), 850–910.

Knoke, D., & Yang, S. (2020). *Social network analysis*. Los Angeles, CA: SAGE.

Koskinen, J., Robins, G. L., Wang, P., & Pattison, P. E. (2013). Bayesian analysis for partially observed network data, missing ties, attributes and actors. *Social Networks*, *35*(4), 514–527.

Koskinen, J., & Snijders, T. A. B. (2007). Bayesian inference for dynamic social network data. *Journal of Statistical Planning and Inference*, *137*(1), 3930–3938.

Kossinets, G. (2006). Effects of missing data in social networks. *Social Networks*, *4*(1), 247–268.

Krause, R. W., Huisman, M., & Snijders, T. A. B. (2018). Multiple imputation for longitudinal network data. *Italian Journal of Applied Statistics*, *30*(1), 33–55.

Krause, R. W., Huisman, M., Steglich, C., & Snijders, T. A. B. (2018). Missing network data: A comparison of different imputation methods. *2018 IEEE/ACM International Conference on Advances in Social Network Analysis and Mining*, 1–5.

Kreager, D. A., Young, J. T. N., Haynie, D. L., Bouchard, M., Schaefer, D. R., & Zajac, G. (2017). Where "old heads" prevail: Inmate hierarchy in a men's prison unit. *American Sociological Review*, *82*(4), 685–718.

Krivitsky, P. N. (2012). Exponential-family random graph models for valued networks. *Electronic Journal of Statistics*, *6*(1), 1100–1128.

Krivitsky, P. N. (2017). Using contrastive divergence to seed Monte Carlo MLE for exponential-family random graph models. *Computational Statistics and Data Analysis*, *107*(C), 149–161.

Krivitsky, P. N., & Butts, C. T. (2017). Exponential-family random graph models for rank-order relational data. *Sociological Methodology*, *47*, 68–112.

Krivitsky, P. N., & Handcock, M. S. (2014). A separable model for dynamic networks. *Journal of the Royal Statistical Society Series B*, *76*, 29–46.

Leal, D. F. (2021). Network inequalities and international migration in the Americas. *American Journal of Sociology*, *126*(5), 1067–1126.

Lee, F., & Butts, C. T. (2018). Mutual assent or unilateral nomination? A performance comparison of intersection and union rules for integrating self-reports of social relationships. *Social Networks*, *55*, 55–62.

Leenders, R. (2002). Modeling social influence through network autocorrelation: Constructing the weight matrix. *Social Networks*, *24*(1), 21–47.

Leifeld, P., & Cranmer, S. (2019). A performance based comparison of the temporal exponential random graph model and stochastic actor oriented model. *Network Science*, *7*(1), 20–51.

Leifeld, P., Cranmer, S. J., & Desmarais, B. A. (2018). Temporal exponential random graph models with btergm: Estimation and bootstrap confidence intervals. *Journal of Statisitcal Software*, *83*, 1–36.

Lerner, J., Bussmann, M., Snijders, T. A. B., & Brandes, U. (2013). Modeling frequency and type of interaction in event networks. *Corvinus Journal of Sociology and Social Policy*, *4*(1), 3–32.

Lerner, J., & Lomi, A. (2020a). The free encyclopedia that anyone can dispute: An analysis of the micro-structural dynamics of positive and negative relations in the production of contentious Wikipedia articles. *Social Networks*, *60*, 11–25.

Lerner, J., & Lomi, A. (2020b). Reliability of relational event model estimates under sampling: How to fit a relational event model to 360 million dyadic events. *Network Science*, *8*(1), 97–135.

Lerner, J., Lomi, A., Mowbray, J., Rollings, N., & Tranmer, M. (2017). Dynamic network analysis of contact diaries. *Social Networks*, *66*(1), 224–236.

Leszczensky, L., & Wolbring, T. (2019). How to deal with reverse causality using panel data? Recommendations for researchers based on a simulation study. *Sociological Methods and Research*, 1–29.

134

Lewis, K., & Kaufman, J. (2018). The conversion of cultural tastes into social network ties. *American Journal of Sociology*, *123*(6), 1684–1742.

Long, J. S., & Mustillo, S. A. (2021). Using predictions and marginal effects to compare groups in regression models for binary outcomes. *Sociological Methods & Research*, *50*, 1284–1320.

Lusher, D., Koskinen, J., & Robins, G. (2013). *Exponential random graph models for social networks*. Cambridge, UK: Cambridge University Press.

Macy, M. (1991). Chains of cooperation: Threshold effects in collective action. *American Sociological Review*, *56*(6), 730–747.

McFadden, D. (1974). Conditional logit analysis of qualitative choice behavior. *Frontiers in Econometrics*, *1*(1), 105–143.

McMillan, C., Felmlee, D., & Braines, D. (2020). Dynamic patterns of terrorist networks: Security versus efficiency in the evolution of eleven islamic extremist attack networks. *Journal of Quantitative Criminology*, *36*(1), 559–581.

McPherson, M. A., & Nieswiadomy, M. L. (2005). Environmental kuznets curve: Threatened species and spatial effects. *Ecological Economics*, *55*(3), 395–407.

Melamed, D., Harrell, A., & Simpson, B. (2018). Cooperation, clustering, and assortative mixing in dynamic networks. *Proceedings of the National Academy of Sciences*, *115*(5), 951–956.

Mize, T., Doan, L., & Long, J. S. (2019). A general framework for comparing predictions and marginal effects across models. *Sociological Methodology*, 1–38.

Mizruchi, M. S., & Neuman, E. J. (2008). The effect of density on the level of bias in the network autocorrelation model. *Social Networks*, *30*(1), 190–200.

Mizruchi, M. S., & Stearns, L. B. (2006). The conditional nature of embeddedness: A study of borrowing by large U.S. firms, 1973–1994. *American Sociological Review*, *71*(2), 310–333.

Mood, C. (2010). Logistic regression: Why we cannot do what we think we can do, and what we can do about it. *European Sociological Review*, *26*(1), 67–82.

Morris, M., Handcock, M. S., & Hunter, D. R. (2008). Specification of exponential-family random graph models: Terms and computational aspects. *Journal of Statistical Software*, *24*(4), 1–22.

Mouw, T. (2006). Estimating the causal effect of social capital: A review of recent research. *Annual Review of Sociology*, *32*(1), 79–102.

Neuman, E. J., & Mizruchi, M. S. (2010). Structure and bias in the network autocorrelation model. *Social Networks*, *32*(1), 290–300.

Newman, M. E. (2010). *Networks: An introduction*. Oxford, UK: Oxford University Press.

Nickell, S. J. (1981). Biases in dynamic models with fixed effects. *Econometrica*, *49*(6), 1417–1426.

Niezink, N. M. D., Snijders, T. A. B., & van Duijn, M. A. J. (2019). No longer discrete: Modeling the dynamics of social network and continuous behavior. *Sociological Methodology*, *49*(1), 295–340.

O'Malley, A. J., Elwert, F., Rosenquist, J. N., Zaslavsky, A. M., & Christakis, N. A. (2014). Estimating peer effects in longitudinal dyadic data using instrumental variables. *Biometrics*, *70*(3), 506–515.

Padgett, J. F., & Ansell, C. K. (1993). Robust action and the rise of the Medici, 1400–1434. *American Journal of Sociology*, *98*, 1259–1319.

Papachristos, A. V., & Bastomski, S. (2018). Connected in crime: The enduring effect of neighborhood networks on the spatial patterning of violence. *American Journal of Sociology*, *124*(2), 517–568.

Papachristos, A. V., Hureau, D. M., & Braga, A. A. (2013). The corner and the crew: The influence of geography and social networks on gang violence. *American Sociological Review*, *78*(3), 417–447.

Perry, P. O., & Wolfe, P. J. (2013). Point process modelling for directed interaction networks. *Journal of the Royal Statistical Society, Series B, Statistical Methodology*, *75*(4), 821–849.

Pink, S., Kretschmer, D., & Leszczensky, L. (2020). Choice modelling in social networks using stochastic actor-oriented models. *Journal of Choice Modeling*, *34*, 1–13.

Podolny, J. (2010). *Status signals: A sociological study of market competition.* Princeton, NJ: Princeton University Press.

Ragan, D. T., Osgood, D. W., & Feinberg, M. E. (2014). Friends as a bridge to parental influence: Implications for adolescent alcohol use. *Social Forces*, *92*(3), 1061–1085.

Ripley, R., Snijders, T. A. B., Boda, Z., Voros, A., & Preciado, P. (2020). *Manual for RSiena.* (Unpublished manuscript)

Robins, G., Pattison, P., Kalish, Y., & Lusher, D. (2007). An introduction to exponential random graph (p*) models for social networks. *Social Networks*, *29*, 173–193.

Robins, G., Pattison, P., & Woolcock, J. (2004). Missing data in networks: Exponential random graph (p*) models for networks with non-respondents. *Social Networks*, *26*(3), 257–283.

Rubin, D. B. (1976). Inference and missing data. *Biometrika*, *63*(1), 581–592.

Schaefer, D. R. (2018). A network analysis of factors leading adolescents to befriend substance-using peers. *Journal of Quantitative Criminology*, *34*(1), 275–312.

Schaefer, D. R., Kornienko, O., & Fox, A. M. (2011). Misery does not love company: Network selection mechanisms and depression homophily. *American Sociological Review*, *76*(5), 764–785.

Schaefer, D. R., & Kreager, D. A. (2020). New on the block: Analyzing network selection trajectories in a prison treatment program. *American Sociological Review*, *85*(4), 709–737.

Schaefer, D. R., & Marcum, C. (2017). Modeling network dynamics. In J. Moody & R. Light (Eds.), *Oxford encyclopedia of social networks* (pp. 254–282). Oxford, UK: Oxford University Press.

Schweinberger, M. (2012). Statistical modelling of network panel data: Goodness of fit. *British Journal of Mathematical and Statistical Psychology*, *65*(2), 263–281.

Schweinberger, M. (2020). Consistent structure estimation of exponential family random graph models with block structure. *Bernoulli*, *26*, 1205–1233.

Schweinberger, M., & Handcock, M. S. (2015). Local dependence in random graph models: Characterization, properties, and statistical inference. *Journal of the Royal Statistical Society, Series B*, *77*, 647–676.

Schweinberger, M., Krivitsky, P. N., Butts, C. T., & Stewart, J. R. (2020). Exponential-family models of random graphs: Inference in finite, super, and infinite population scenarios. *Statistical Science*, *35*(4), 627–662.

Schweinberger, M., & Stewart, J. R. (2020). Concentration and consistency results for canonical and curved exponential-family models of random graphs. *The Annals of Statistics*, *48*(1), 374–396.

Shalizi, C. R., & Thomas, A. C. (2011). Homophily and contagion are generically confounded in observational social network studies. *Sociological Methods and Research*, *40*(2), 211–239.

Smith, J., & Moody, J. (2013). Network sampling coverage I: Nodes missing at random. *Social Networks*, *35*, 652–668.

Smith, J., Moody, J., & Morgan, J. (2017). Network sampling coverage II: The effect of non-random missing data on network measurements. *Social Networks*, *48*(1), 78–99.

Snijders, T. A. B. (1996). Stochastic actor-oriented models for network change. *Journal of Mathematical Sociology*, *21*, 149–172.

Snijders, T. A. B. (2001). The statistical evaluation of social network dynamics. *Sociological Methodology*, *31*(1), 361–395.

Snijders, T. A. B. (2002). Markov chain Monte Carlo estimation of exponential random graph models. *Journal of Social Structure*, *3*, 1–40.

Snijders, T. A. B. (2017). Stochastic actor-oriented models for network dynamics. *Annual Review of Statistics and Its Application*, *4*(1), 343–363.

Snijders, T. A. B., Koskinen, J., & Schweinberger, M. (2010). Maximum likelihood estimation for social network dynamics. *Annals of Applied Statistics*, *4*(1), 567–588.

Snijders, T. A. B., & Lomi, A. (2019). Beyond homophily: Incorporating actor variables in statistical network models. *Network Science*, *7*(1), 1–19.

Snijders, T. A. B., Lomi, A., & Torló, V. J. (2013). A model for the multiplex dynamics of two-mode and one-mode networks, with an application to employment preference, friendship, and advice. *Social Networks*, *35*(2), 265–276.

Snijders, T. A. B., Pattison, P. E., Robins, G. L., & Handcock, M. S. (2006). New specifications for exponential random graph models. *Sociological Methodology*, *36*(1), 99–150.

Snijders, T. A. B., Steglich, C., & Schweinberger, M. (2007). Modeling the coevolution of networks and behavior. In H. O. Montfort & A. Satorra (Eds.), *Longitudinal models in the behavioral and related sciences* (p. 41-71). Mahwah, NJ: Lawrence Erlbaum.

Snijders, T. A. B., & Steglich, C. E. G. (2015). Representing micro-macro linkages by actor-based dynamic network models. *Sociological Methods & Research*, *44*(2), 222–271.

Snijders, T. A. B., van de Bunt, G. G., & Steglich, C. E. (2010). Introduction to stochastic actor-based models for network dynamics. *Social Networks*, *32*(1), 44–60.

Stadfeld, C., Snijders, T. A. B., Steglich, C., & van Duijn, M. (2020). Statistical power in longitudinal network studies. *Sociological Methods and Research*, *49*(4), 1103–1132.

Stadtfeld, C., & Block, P. (2017). Interactions, actors, and time: Dynamic network actor models for relational events. *Sociological Science*, *4*(1), 318–352.

Stadtfeld, C., Hollway, J., & Block, P. (2017a). Dynamic network actor models: Investigating coordination ties through time. *Sociological Methodology*, *47*(1), 1–40.

Stadtfeld, C., Hollway, J., & Block, P. (2017b). Rejoinder: Dynams and the grounds for actor-oriented network event models. *Sociological Methodology*, *47*(1), 56–67.

Steglich, C., Snijders, T. A. B., & Pearson, M. (2010). Dynamic networks and behavior: Separating selection from influence. *Sociological Methodology*, *40*(1), 329–393.

Stewart, J., Schweinberger, M., Bojanowski, M., & Morris, M. (2019). Multilevel network data facilitate statistical inference for curved ERGMs with geometrically weighted terms. *Social Networks*, *59*, 98–119.

Stivala, A., Garry, R., & Lomi, A. (2020). Exponential random graph model parameter estimation for very large directed networks. *PLoS One*, *15*(1), 1–21.

Strauss, D., & Ikeda, M. (1990). Pseudolikelihood estimation for social networks. *Journal of the American Statistical Association*, *85*(409), 204–212.

Sutherland, E. (1939). *Principles of criminology* (2nd ed.). Philadelphia, PA: Lippincott.

Thiemichen, S., Friel, N., Caimo, A., & Kauermann, G. (2016). Bayesian exponential random graph models with nodal random effects. *Social Networks*, *46*, 11–28.

Tita, G., & Radil, S. M. (2011). Spatializing the social networks of gangs to explore patterns of violence. *Journal of Quantitative Criminology*, *27*(4), 307–332.

Turanovic, J. J., & Young, J. T. (2016). Violent offending and victimization in adolescence: Social network mechanisms and homophily. *Criminology*, *54*(3), 487–519.

137

Vaisey, S., & Miles, A. (2017). What you can—and can't—do with three wave panel data. *Sociological Methods and Research*, *46*(1), 44–67.

Valente, T. W. (1995). *Network models of the diffusion of innovations*. New York, NY: Hampton Press.

Van De Bunt, G. G., Duijn, M. A. J. V., & Snijders, T. A. B. (1999). Friendship networks through time: An actor-oriented dynamic statistical network model. *Computational and Mathematical Organization Theory*, *5*(2), 167–192.

van Duijn, M. A., Snijders, T. A. B., & Zijlstra, B. J. H. (2004). p2: A random effects model with covariates for directed graphs. *Statistica Neerlandica*, *58*(2), 234–254.

Vega Yon, G. G., Slaughter, A., & de la Haye, K. (2021). Exponential random graph models for little networks. *Social Networks*, *64*, 225–238.

Wang, P., Sharpe, K., Robins, G. L., & Pattison, P. E. (2009). Exponential random graph (p*) models for affiliation networks. *Social Networks*, *31*, 12–25.

Wasserman, S., & Faust, K. (1994). *Social network analysis: Methods and applications*. Cambridge, UK: Cambridge University Press.

Watts, D. J. (2002). A simple model of global cascades on random networks. *Proceedings of the National Academy of Sciences*, *99*(9), 5766–5771.

Watts, D. J., & Strogatz, S. H. (1998). Collective dynamics of 'small-world' networks. *Nature*, *393*, 440–442.

Weerman, F. M. (2011). Delinquent peers in context: A longitudinal network analysis of selection and influence effects. *Criminology*, *49*(1), 253–286.

Wiersema, M. F., & Bowen, H. P. (2009). The use of limited dependent variable techniques in strategy research: Issues and methods. *Strategic Management Journal*, *30*(6), 679–692.

Wooldridge, J. (2002). *Econometric Analysis of Cross Section and Panel Data*. Cambridge: MIT Press.

Yang, S., Keller, F. B., & Lu, Z. (2016). *Social network analysis: Methods and examples*. Los Angeles, CA: SAGE.

Young, J. T. N. (2014). A sensitivity analysis of egocentric measures of peer delinquency to latent homophily: A research note. *Journal of Quantitative Criminology*, *30*(1), 373–387.

INDEX